PROPHETIC
MINISTRY

A Classic Study on the Nature of a Prophet

PROPHETIC
MINISTRY

A Classic Study on the Nature of a Prophet

T. AUSTIN SPARKS

Published by MercyPlace Ministries

MercyPlace is a licensed imprint of Destiny Image®, Inc.

Destiny Image® Publishers, Inc.
P.O. Box 310
Shippensburg, PA 17257-0310

ISBN 0-9677402-4-X
(previously ISBN 0-7684-4000-9)

For Worldwide Distribution
Printed in the U.S.A.

This book and all other Destiny Image, Revival Press, MercyPlace, Fresh Bread, and Treasure House books are available at Christian bookstores and distributors worldwide.

For a U.S. bookstore nearest you, call **1-800-722-6774**.
For more information on foreign distributors, call **717-532-3040**.
Or reach us on the Internet: **http://www.reapernet.com**

CONTENTS

ENDORSEMENT
By Dr. Bill Hamon
Christian International Ministries Network

T. Austin Sparks has pioneered the need for prophets and prophetic ministry. He declared, "The crying need for our time is for a prophetic ministry—a voice that interprets the mind of God to people." That statement is as true today as it was in his day. Those who desire to fulfill the scriptural command to "covet prophetic ministry" need to read this book. It reveals not only the characteristics of prophetic ministry, but also the character God desires for all who would be true demonstrators of His prophetic ministry.

PUBLISHER'S NOTE

OVER THE LAST 17 YEARS I have had the honor of publishing some of the most anointed prophetic voices in our land. These men and women have cried out for a return to God's ultimate intentions and for a resurgence of His presence in our midst.

I have always had a passionate attraction to the prophetic ministry. Prophets have been something of a despised lot. It seems as though they gain popularity only after they have died. Misunderstood and rarely appreciated, the prophet stands in the gap seeking to give birth to the word of the Lord. We desperately need more prophets cut out of that mold. I have the opportunity to reach back in time and introduce to you a man born out of due season, T. Austin Sparks. Sparks was one of those men who had an intense desire for the 'word of the Lord.' He was truly a man hidden away in his generation.

It is my great joy to make his classic writing on the prophetic available to a new generation that is hungry to be God's representatives on the earth. *Prophetic Ministry* is a must-read for everyone who would dare to speak on God's behalf. As the Publisher, it is my prayer that this prophetic word will kindle a fresh flame in your heart.

—Don Nori

PICTURE OF A PROPHET

THE PROPHET IN HIS DAY is fully accepted of God and totally rejected by men.

Years back, Dr. Gregory Mantle was right when he said, "No man
can be fully accepted until he is totally rejected." The prophet of the Lord
is aware of both of these experiences. They are his "brand name."

The group, challenged by the prophet because they are smug and
comfortably insulated from a perishing world in their warm but untested
theology, is not likely to vote him "Man of the year" when he refers to
them as habituates of the synagogue of Satan!

The prophet comes to set up that which is upset. His work is to call
into line those who are out of line! He is unpopular because he opposes
the popular in morality and spirituality. In a day of faceless politicians
and voiceless preachers, there is not a more urgent national need than
that we cry to God for a prophet! The function of the prophet, as Austin
Sparks once said, "has almost always been that of recovery."

The prophet is God's detective seeking for a lost treasure. The
degree of his effectiveness is determined by his measure of unpopularity.
Compromise is not known to him.

He has no price tags.
He is totally "otherworldly."
He is unquestionably controversial and unpardonably hostile.

He marches to another drummer!

He breathes the rarefied air of inspiration.

He is a "seer" who comes to lead the blind.

He lives in the heights of God and comes into the valley with a "thus saith the Lord."

He shares some of the foreknowledge of God and so is aware of impending judgment.

He lives in "splendid isolation."

He is forthright and outright, but he claims no birthright.

His message is "repent, be reconciled to God or else...!"

His prophecies are parried.

His truth brings torment, but his voice is never void.

He is the villain of today and the hero of tomorrow.

He is excommunicated while alive and exalted when dead!

He is dishonored with epithets when breathing and honored with epitaphs when dead.

He is a schoolmaster to bring us to Christ, but few "make the grade" in his class.

He is friendless while living and famous when dead.

He is against the establishment in ministry; then he is established as a saint by posterity.

He eats daily the bread of affliction while he ministers, but he feeds the Bread of Life to those who listen.

He walks before men for days but has walked before God for years.

He is a scourge to the nation before he is scourged by the nation.

He announces, pronounces, and denounces!

He has heart like a volcano and his words are as fire.

He talks to men about God.

He carries the lamp of truth amongst heretics while he is lampooned by men.

He faces God before he faces men, but he is self-effacing.

He hides with God in the secret place, but he has nothing to hide in the marketplace.

He is naturally sensitive but supernaturally spiritual.

He has passion, purpose and pugnacity.

He is ordained of God but disdained by men.

Our national need at this hour is not that the dollar recover its strength, or that we save face over the Watergate affair, or that we find the answer to the ecology problem. We need a God-sent prophet!

I am bombarded with talk or letters about the coming shortages in our national life: bread, fuel, energy. I read between the lines from people not practiced in scaring folk. They feel that the "seven years of plenty" are over for us. The "seven years of famine" are ahead. But the greatest famine of all in this nation at this given moment is a FAMINE OF THE HEARING OF THE WORDS OF GOD (Amos 8:11).

Millions have been spent on evangelism in the last twenty-five years. Hundreds of gospel messages streak through the air over the nation every day. Crusades have been held; healing meetings have made a vital contribution. "Come-outers" have "come out" and settled, too, without a nation-shaking revival. Organizers we have. Skilled preachers abound. Multi-million dollar Christian organizations straddle the nation. BUT where, oh where, is the prophet? Where are the incandescent men fresh from the holy place? Where is the Moses to plead in fasting before the holiness of the Lord for our moldy morality, our political perfidy, and sour and sick spirituality?

GOD'S MEN ARE IN HIDING UNTIL THE DAY OF THEIR SHOWING FORTH. They will come. The prophet is violated during his ministry, but he is vindicated by history.

There is a terrible vacuum in evangelical Christianity today. The missing person in our ranks is the prophet. The man with a terrible earnestness. The man totally otherworldly. The man rejected by other men, even other good men, because they consider him too austere, too severely committed, too negative and unsociable.

Let him be as plain as John the Baptist.
Let him for a season be a voice crying in the wilderness of modern theology and stagnant "churchianity."
Let him be as selfless as Paul the apostle.
Let him, too, say and live, "This ONE thing I do."
Let him reject ecclesiastical favors.

Let him be self-abasing, nonself-seeking, nonself-projecting, nonself-righteous, nonself-glorying, nonself-promoting.

Let him say nothing that will draw men to himself but only that which will move men to God.

Let him come daily from the throne room of a holy God, the place where he has received the order of the day.

Let him, under God, unstop the ears of the millions who are deaf through the clatter of shekels milked from this hour of material mesmerism.

Let him cry with a voice this century has not heard because he has seen a vision no man in this century has seen. God send us this Moses to lead us from the wilderness of crass materialism, where the rattlesnakes of lust bite us and where enlightened men, totally blind spiritually, lead us to an ever-nearing Armageddon.

God have mercy! Send us PROPHETS!

Leonard Ravenhill
Used by permission of Martha Ravenhill

FOREWORD

ASK ANY MINISTER "Where's a good place to eat around here?" and he will quickly list off a plethora of options—from his favorite steak house or Chinese buffet to the best Italian or Mexican restaurant in town.

My late father, Leonard Ravenhill, was not a connoisseur of fine cuisine. He did however have a keen nose for finding the "finest of the wheat" from which to satisfy his spiritual hunger for solid revelation and insight into God's word. When I was a young man on the mission field, my father would send me boxes of books that included a variety of writings from T. Austin Sparks. These are now a cherished part of my own personal library. After 35 years of ministry, I too can recommend to the next generation, that these writings are a "must" if they are going to effectively "serve the purpose of God in their generation."

Several years ago, my wife and I gazed in awe at one of the greatest art works in history, the ceiling of the Sistine Chapel in Rome. This incredible fresco by Michelangelo had just been painstakingly restored by a process that had taken many years. Prior to this restoration, art historians had declared Michelangelo to be one of the greatest sculptors of all time, but said that he was an artist who "painted with a dark palette." Following its completion in 1509, this incredible masterpiece had suffered the devastating effects of carbon soot that had ascended from the numerous candles and lamps used to light this magnificent chapel. The

PROPHETIC MINISTRY

November 1991 issue of *Life* magazine carried this headline on its cover: "First pictures of Michelangelo's Sistine Chapel as it hasn't been seen in five hundred years—A CLEAR VIEW OF HEAVEN." The restoration, finally completed, revealed for the first time in centuries the blaze of brilliant and vivid colors. Suddenly, this once drab fresco now confounded and embarrassed the experts who had concocted their own theories of its dark look.

Likewise, the writings of T. Austin Sparks strip away the centuries of misunderstanding that have caused us to accept the Church in her present condition. In this spiritual masterpiece, the writer seeks to recover God's original intention for His Church. This, says Sparks, is the true essence of prophetic ministry. This book is not a handbook on personal prophecy, but rather, an insightful look at the true nature of the prophetic— that of "recovering the Lord's testimony in fulness."

How I long for this day of restoration, when once again God reveals His workmanship in all her radiant glory, as the world watches in embarrassment and awe. I pray that as you read this book, the eyes of your understanding will be opened afresh and you'll never again be satisfied to make the excuse that God painted "with a dark palette." Reserve for yourself a quiet corner in the "restaurant of the Spirit" and feast at this succulent table of wisdom and revelation. Allow the strength of this meat to sustain, strengthen, and enliven you as you seek to co-labor with Christ in "recovering His testimony in fulness."

—David Ravenhill, author
They Drank From the River and Died in the Wilderness,
and *For God's Sake, Grow Up!*

BIOGRAPHY

T. Austin Sparks, 1888-1971

THEODORE AUSTIN SPARKS was a native of south London, educated there and in Scotland. His father moved in the musical world and had little time for God, but from his mother's side he inherited a long tradition of evangelical Christian faith handed down among Baptists of a Suffolk farming community. He himself however remained unmoved by the Spirit of God until one night, at the age of 17, he was suddenly arrested by the earnest preaching of the gospel in the cold open air of a Glasgow street. That night he went back to his room and gave his life to the Lord. It was a committal from which he never withdrew.

Started in business in Glasgow he engaged also in children's missions and slum work, and gathered a group of friends for Bible study in his home. Soon also he felt the call of God to proclaim the good news of redemption in several small mission halls, there and in and around London. Sensing that he might have a gift from God in this field, but lacking the means to secure a formal training for the ministry, he did the next best thing; he began to read widely, and used his free time to go and hear some of the last of the great turn-of-the-century preachers and Bible expositors. Notable among these were Dr. G. Campbell Morgan of Westminster Chapel, London, and F.B. Meyer, who was to become a firm friend and counsellor. His devotion to God had begun to be recognised and at the age of 25 he was unanimously called to serve a congregational church in

Stoke Newington, north of the Thames. He accepted the pastorate at a time when the church was at a low ebb, and was to leave them nine years later, "well-instructed and firmly founded on the ever-enduring truths of the gospel of Jesus Christ." While there, in 1915, he married Florence Rowland, daughter of godly parents, who from then was to prove his life-long support and spiritual companion.

From Stoke Newington he moved on in 1921 to the charge of Honor Oak Baptist Church in an undistinguished south-east London suburb. It was while here that he began to be more widely known as a gifted and original minister of the Word. His health was never good, but backed by a faithful praying group in his own church he began to travel more widely in Britain. In 1925 he paid a first visit to the United States as speaker at a Victorious Life Conference in Keswick Grove, New Jersey. He had begun to see, perhaps more clearly than many of his contemporaries, that the cross of Christ is central, not only to world history but also to human experience. To "lose his life" is the disciple's safe but costly way of entry to a service that is marked by eternal gain, and the discovery of this fact explains and gives meaning to so much in life that the Christian otherwise finds difficult. One day in his study, while waiting on God for the needs of His flock, the truth that "it is no longer I, but Christ who lives in me" dawned freshly upon him with compelling power. Afterwards he often spoke of the "open heaven" beneath which, from that day on, he ministered.

The Baptist congregation grew, but, with his emphasis on the Christian's walk of faith, so too did dissatisfaction with what his deacons began to see as materialist methods of fund-raising favoured at that time by the British Baptist Union who held the church property. Thus it came about that in 1926 they, together with almost the whole congregation, supported a move to a vacant rented property—a school hall and residence—in the same general locality of Honor Oak. His lately redesigned church magazine *A Witness and a Testimony* continued from the new address to be issued bi-monthly, free of subscription, with a modest but increasingly worldwide circulation through until his death in 1971.

The New Christian Fellowship Centre, with its thriving local church and regular week-end conferences and its occasional longer training sessions for young men, became a place of pilgrimage for many. In 1931 this was supplemented by a Scottish summer Conference Centre on the Firth of Clyde at the well-situated house of Heathfield, Kilcreggan. Meanwhile others of like vision had joined him in the ministry. He had dropped the title "The Reverend," and they shared an ideal of ministers and elders working "together in unity"; though always his unquestioned gift of preaching set him a little apart. A small press was started for publication of the magazine and of collections of his largely unedited spoken messages.

Down the years there were developments in emphasis in the ministry of the Word, "as", in his words, "there should ever be where there is life and growth, provided that the essential foundation remains true and unchanging." So the gospel was faithfully preached, but with it there was a strong emphasis for believers on the life in the Spirit, the eternal purpose of God in His Son, the Christian's spiritual warfare, and the heavenly nature, vocation and destiny of the Church, the Body of Christ.

This last emphasis on a Church-based witness worldwide meant effectually that the missionary vision of the local church at Honor Oak found strong encouragement from, and sympathy with, the rising indigenous movements of the Spirit of God overseas that, for a while during the thirties and forties, seemed a problem to leaders of the old-established missionary societies. As a consequence church prayer meetings, always a mainspring of the local testimony at Honor Oak, now ranged in vision over a wide area of the work of God in the earth. Missionaries went forth to work in fellowship alongside such movements, and Mr. Austin Sparks himself was privileged to travel widely in ministry, not only in Europe and North America but also further afield in India and the Far East. Such opportunities for fellowship with those in whom the Spirit of God was doing His own original work were to afford him lifelong joy.

From his early years he had believed in the power and significance of the spoken Word of God, and that all developments of its exposition and application should be vitally related to the actual and growing needs of the spiritual life of representative bodies of God's people. Through His Word God would meet His own, but His way of giving to His servants was not merely through bookish, cloistered or studied matter. Rather it was made necessary, drawn out and given meaning by the call and answer of living conditions. Its value—if it was to be anything more than words—lay in its being able to touch the Lord's people at the point of experience and need which had been the occasion of its original calling forth.

Such was the special calling of T. Austin Sparks, a man ploughing a furrow perhaps a little apart from his contemporaries, but always true to Christ Jesus his Saviour and Lord, and committed to a vision of spiritually fruitful harvests throughout the whole field that is God's world.

A.I.K., October 1983
(As submitted by David Ravenhill,
from the library of his late father, Leonard Ravenhill)

INTRODUCTION

THE FUNCTION OF THE PROPHET has almost invariably been that of recovery. That implies that his business related to something lost. That something being absolutely essential to God's full satisfaction, the dominant note of the Prophet was one of dissatisfaction. And, there being the additional factor that, for obvious reasons, the people were not disposed to go the costly way of God's full purpose, the Prophet was usually an unpopular person.

But his unpopularity was no proof of his being wrong or unnecessary, for every Prophet was eventually vindicated, though with very great suffering and shame to the people.

If it be true that prophetic ministry is related to the need for the recovery of God's full thought as to His people, surely this is a time of such need! Few honest and thoughtful people will contend that things are all well with the Church of Christ to-day. A brief comparison with the first years of the Church's life will bring out a vivid contrast between then and the *centuries* since.

Take alone the lifetime of one man—Paul.

In the year 33 A.D. a few unknown men, looked upon as poor and ignorant, were associated with one 'Jesus of Nazareth'—which very designation was despicable in the minds of all reputable and influential people. These men, after that Jesus had been crucified, were later found seeking to proclaim His Lordship and Saviourhood, but were handled hardly by all official bodies.

In the year that Paul died—67-68 A.D. (34 years later)—how did the matter stand? There were churches in Jerusalem, Nazareth, Caesarea; Antioch and all Syria; Galatia; Sardis, Laodicea, Ephesus and all the towns on the West coast throughout lesser Asia; in Philippi, Thessalonica, Athens, Corinth, and the chief cities of the islands and the mainland of Greece; Rome, and the Western Roman Colonies; and in Alexandria.

The history of *generations* of missionary enterprise, tens of thousands of missionaries, vast sums of money, immense administrative organizations, and much more on the publicity, propaganda, and advocacy side, does not compare at all favourably with the above. We now find ourselves confronted by the end of the whole system of world missions and professional missionaries *as they have existed for a very long time*, and still the world is not evangelized.

Is there a reason for this? We feel—nay, know—that there is. The explanation is not in a difference in Divine purpose or Divine willingness to support that purpose. It is in the difference in apprehension of the basis, way, and object of the work of God.

Some proof of this is recognisable in our own time. In much less than the lifetime of one man in China, churches of a deeply spiritual character sprang into being all over that land; four hundred of them in a few years. At the time when Communism overran that country a movement was in progress which was not only covering China, but reaching beyond, and as a result living churches are now found in many other parts of the Far East. This was for years a despised, persecuted, and much ostracised work. But since missionary movements and societies have had to leave the country this work has gone on, and, although with many martyrs, is still going on. The man raised up of God lies in prison, but the work is unarrested.

The same kind of thing is taking place in India, and in only a very few years of the life of one God-apprehended man churches of a real New Testament character have come into being all over the country and beyond. The opposition is very great, but the work is of God, and cannot be stopped.

What, again is, the explanation?

The answer is not to be found in the realm of zeal or devotion to the salvation of souls. Rather is it this: that there was at the beginning the supreme factor of an absolutely original and new apprehension of Christ and God's eternal purpose concerning Him. This *revelation* by the Holy Spirit came with devastating and revolutionising power to the Apostles and the Church, and, rather than being a 'tradition handed down from the fathers,' a ready-made system, all set and entered into as such, it was, for every one of them, as though it had only newly dropped from heaven —which, in fact, was true.

This movement of God, brought about by a mighty upheaving of all traditions and 'old' things by a practical experience of the Cross, was marked by three features: —

(1) Utter heavenliness and spirituality;

(2) Universality, involving the negation of all prejudices, exclusiveness and partiality; and

(3) The utter Lordship and Headship of Christ *directly* operating by the sovereignty of the Holy Spirit.

This was all gathered into a tremendous and overpowering initial and progressive realisation of the immense significance of Christ in the eternal counsels of God, and therefore of the Church as His Body. Anything that corresponds to the results which characterized the beginning will—and does—correspond to the reason, namely, a getting back behind tradition, the set and established system, institutionalism, ecclesiasticism, commercialism, organizationalism, etc., to a virgin, original, new breaking upon the consciousness of God's full thought concerning His Son.

To bring into view this *full* purpose of God was the essence of the Prophet's ministry, and will always be so. We may not now speak of a special class as 'Prophets,' but the function may still be operative, and it is function that matters more than office.

Forest Hill, London.
June, 1954   T.A.S.

ONE

WHAT PROPHETIC MINISTRY IS

Reading: Deuteronomxy viii. 15, 18; Acts iii. 22; vii. 37; Luke xxiv. 19; Revelation xix. 10; Ephesians iv. 8, 11–13.

"He gave some...prophets...for the perfecting of the saints, unto the work of ministering, unto the building up of the body of Christ" (Ephesians iv. 11, 12).

WE ARE GOING TO CONSIDER the matter of prophetic ministry. "He gave some...prophets." But we must at once make some discrimination, for when we speak of prophetic ministry, we find that people are very largely governed by a certain mentality associated with what is called 'prophecy.' They immediately relate the very term 'prophetic' to incidents, happenings, dates, and so on, lying mainly in the future. That is, they think instantly of the predictive element in prophetic ministry and limit the whole function to that conception.

Now, for the real value of what is before us we must remove from our minds that restricted idea of the preeminence of the predictive aspect in prophetic ministry. It is an aspect, but it is only an aspect. Prophetic ministry is a much larger thing than the predictive.

Perhaps it would be better if we said that the prophetic *function*, going far beyond mere events, happenings and dates, is the ministry of spiritual interpretation. That phrase will cover the whole ground of that with which we are now concerned. Prophecy is spiritual interpretation. If you think about it for a moment, in the light of prophetic ministry in the Word of God, I am quite sure you will see how true this is. It is the interpretation of everything from a spiritual standpoint; the bringing of the spiritual implications of things, past, present and future, before the people of God, and giving them to understand the significance of things in their spiritual value and meaning. That was and is the essence of prophetic ministry.

Of course, what we know about prophets in the Scriptures is that they were a special function or faculty amongst the Lord's people, but we must also remember that they often combined their prophetic function with other functions. Samuel was a prophet; he was also a judge, and a priest. Moses was a prophet, but he was other things besides. I believe Paul was a prophet; he was an apostle, an evangelist; he was everything, it seems to me! So that our purpose is to speak not so much of *prophets*, as distinct people, as of prophetic *ministry*. It is the ministry with which we are concerned, and we shall arrive at the instrument better by recognising the ministry fulfilled; we shall understand the vessel better and see what it is, if we see the purpose for which it is constituted. So let me say that it is function, not persons, that we have in view when we are speaking about prophets or prophetic ministry.

I am quite sure that those who have any knowledge whatever of the times, spiritually, will agree with me when I say that the crying need of our time is for a prophetic ministry. There never was a time when there existed so extensively the need for a voice of interpretation, when conditions needed more the ministry of explanation. One does not want to make extravagant statements or to be extreme in one's utterances, but I do not think it would be either extravagant or extreme to say that the world today is well-nigh bankrupt of real prophetic ministry in this sense—a voice that interprets the mind of God to people. It may exist in some small degree here and there, but in no very large way is that ministry being fulfilled. So often our hearts groan and cry out, Oh, that the mind of God about the present situation could be brought through, in the first place to the recognition of His people, and then through His people to others beyond! There is a great and terrible need for a prophetic ministry in our time.

PROPHETIC MINISTRY RELATED
TO THE FULL PURPOSE OF GOD

Recognising that, we must come to see exactly what this function is. What is the function of prophetic ministry? It is to hold things to the full thought of God, and therefore it is usually a reactionary thing. We usually find that the prophets arose as a reaction from God to the course and drift of things amongst His people; a call back, a re-declaration, a re-pronouncement of God's mind, a bringing into clear view again of the thoughts of God. The prophets stood in the midst of the stream—usually a fast-rushing stream—like a rock; the course of things broke over them. They challenged and resisted that course, and their presence in the midst of the stream represented God's mind as against the prevailing course of things. In the Old Testament, the prophet usually came into his ministry at a time when things were spiritually bad and anything but according to the Divine mind; the state was evil, things were confused, mixed, chaotic; there was much deception and falsehood, and often things very much worse than that. Here is the thing to which the prophetic ministry all- inclusively relates—the original and ultimate purpose of God in and through His people; and when you have said that, you have got right to the heart of

– 3 – .

things. We ask again, What is the prophetic ministry, what is the prophetic function, to what does it relate?—and the answer all-inclusively is that it relates to the full, original and ultimate purpose of God in and through His people.

If that statement is true, it helps us at once to see the need in our time; for, speaking generally, the people of God on the earth in our time have confused parts of the purpose of God with the whole; have emphasized phases to the detriment of the whole. They are confusing means and methods and enthusiasm and zeal with the exact object of the Lord, failing to recognise that God's purpose must be reached in God's way and by God's means, and the way and the means are just as important as the purpose: that is, you cannot reach God's end just anyhow, by any kind of method that you may employ, by projecting your own ideas or programmes or schemes to get to God's end. God has His own way and means of getting to His end. God's thoughts extend to and spread over the smallest detail of His purpose, and you cannot wholly realise the purpose of God except as the very details are according to the mind of God.

God might have said to Moses, Build me a tabernacle, will you? I leave it to you how you do it, what you use; you see what I am after; go and make me a tabernacle. Moses might have got the idea of what God wanted and have worked out the kind of thing he would make for God according to his own mind. But we know that God did not leave a single detail, a peg or a pin's point, a stitch or a thread, to the mind of man. I only use that illustration in order to enforce what I mean, that prophetic ministry is to present God's full, original and ultimate purpose, as it is according to His mind, and hold it like that for God; to interpret the mind of God in all matters concerning the purpose of God, to bring all details into line with the purpose, and to make the purpose govern everything.

PROPHETIC MINISTRY BY THE ANOINTING

(a) DETAILED KNOWLEDGE OF GOD'S PURPOSES

This involves several things which are clearly seen to be features of prophetic ministry in the Word of God. First of all, it involves the matter of anointing. The meaning and value of anointing is that, firstly, only the Spirit of God has the full and detailed plan in view and can make everything to be true in principle to God's intention. I say only the Spirit of God has that. It is one of the most wonderful things in Scripture, to find that, when you get back to the simplest, earliest—shall we say, the most elementary—expression or projecting of Divine things in the Word of God, everything there is so true in principle to all that comes out later in that connection in greater fulness. It is simply marvellous how God has kept everything true to principle: you never find later, however fully a thing is developed, that there is a change in principle; the principle is there and you cannot get away from it. When you later take up a more developed matter in the Word of God you find that it is true to the original principle of that matter as it was first introduced.

And God has brought everything into line with those fixed principles. God does not deviate one little bit. His law is there and it is unchanging. The Holy Spirit alone knows all that. He knows the laws and the principles, all the things which spiritually govern the purpose of God; and He alone knows the plan and the details, and can make everything true to those principles and laws. And everything has got to be true to them. We may take it as settled that if in the superstructure there is anything that is out of harmony with God's original basic spiritual principle, that is going to be a defect which will spell tragedy sooner or later. The superstructure, in every detail of principle, has to be true to the foundation, to the original. Most of us are not enlightened as to all that. We are feeling our way along, we are groping onward, we are getting light, slowly, very little at a time; but we are getting light. But the prophetic ministry is an enlightened ministry, and is that which, under the anointing, is to bring things back to that position of absolute safety and security because it is true to Divine principle.

The anointing is necessary, firstly, because only the Spirit of God is acquainted with all the thought of God and He alone can speak and work and bring things about in true and utter consistency with the Divine principles which govern everything; and everything that is from God must embody those principles. The principle of the Church—that which governs the Church—is that it is a heavenly thing. It is not an earthly thing; it is related to Christ as in heaven. The Church does not come into being until Christ is in heaven, which means that the Church has to come, as to

Christ in heaven, on to heavenly ground, in a spiritual way. It has got to leave earthly ground and really be a heavenly, spiritual thing, while still here, in relation to Christ in heaven. That is a Divine law and principle which is so clear in the New Testament. It is there from "Acts" onward most manifestly.

But this is not something new which has come in with the New Testament. God has put that law into everything that points in any prophetic way to the Church and to Christ. Isaac was not allowed to leave the land and go abroad to fetch his wife. He had to stay there and the servant had to be sent to bring her to where he was. There is your law. Christ is in heaven; the Spirit is sent to bring the Church to where He is—firstly in a spiritual way, and then later literally; but the principle is there. Joseph passes through rejection and typical death and eventually reaches the throne, and with his exaltation he receives his wife, Asenath. Joseph is a clear figure of Christ. It is *on His exaltation* that Christ receives His Church, His Bride. Pentecost is really the result of the exaltation of Christ, when the Church is spiritually brought into living relationship with Himself, the exalted Christ. There is your principle in the simple story of Joseph. You can go on like that, seeing how God in simple details has kept everything true to principle; you find His eternal principles are embodied in the simplest things of the Old Testament, fulfilling this final declaration that the testimony of Jesus is the very spirit of prophecy (Rev. xix. 10). There is something there indicative of a great heavenly truth, which is the spirit of prophecy pointing to Christ.

I wonder whether you have really been impressed with the tremendous importance of Divine principle in things. There is a principle, and the recognition and the honouring of that principle determines the success of the whole. Now, only the Holy Spirit knows all those Divine principles, only He knows the mind of God, the thoughts of God, in fulness. Hence, if things are to be held to the full thought and purpose of God, it can only be under an anointing—which means that the Spirit of God has come to take charge. An anointed ministry means that God the Holy Spirit has become responsible for the whole thing; He has committed Himself to it. I do not suppose anyone would dispute or challenge the statement of the need for the Holy Spirit, the need for Him to be in charge, for everything to be done by Him. But oh, that means a great deal more than a general truth and a general position.

(b) KNOWLEDGE IMPARTED BY REVELATION

It leads to this second thing in prophetic ministry: By the anointing there comes revelation. We can accept in a general way the necessity of the Holy Spirit's doing everything—initiating, conducting, governing and being the power and inspiration of everything; But oh! that is a life-long education, and it brings in the necessity for everything to be given by revelation. That is why the prophets originally were called "seers"—men who saw. They saw what no other men saw. They saw what it was impossible for other people to see, even religious, God-fearing people. They saw by revelation.

A prophetic ministry demands revelation; it is a ministry by revelation. Later we shall examine that more closely, but I want just to emphasize the fact at this moment. I am not thinking now of revelation extra to the Scriptures. I cannot take the ground of certain 'prophets' (?) in the Church to-day who prophesy extra to the Scriptures. No, but within the revelation already given—and God knows it is big enough!—the Holy Spirit yet moves to reveal what 'eye hath not seen, ear hath not heard.'

That is the wonder of a life in the Spirit. It is a life of constant new discovery; everything is full of surprise and wonder. A life under the Holy Spirit can never be static; it can never reach finality here, nor come to the place where the sum of truth is boxed. A life really in the Holy Spirit is a life which realises that there is infinitely, transcendently, more beyond than all we have yet seen or grasped or sensed. People who *know*, who have come to a fixed place and cannot see—let alone move—beyond their present position, represent a position that is foreign to the mind of the Holy Ghost. Prophetic ministry under the Holy Spirit is a ministry through growing revelation.

A prophet was a man who went back to God again and again, and did not come out to speak until God had shown him the next thing. He did not just go on in his professional office because he was a prophet and it was expected of him. There was nothing professional about his position. When it became professional, then tragedy overtook the prophetic office. It did become professional through the 'schools of the prophets' set up by Samuel. We must not even confuse these schools of the prophets with true prophetical office. There was a difference between those who graduated in the schools of the prophets and the true prophets represented by such men as Samuel, Elijah, Elisha. Whenever things become professional, something is lost, because the very essence and

> **It is the nature of revelation to keep things alive and fresh, and filled with Divine energy.**

nature of prophetic ministry is that it is coming by revelation afresh every time. A thing revealed is new; it may be an old thing, but it has about it something that is fresh as a revelation to the heart of the one concerned, and it is so new and wonderful that the effect with him is as though no one had ever yet seen that, although thousands may have seen it before. It is the nature of revelation to keep things alive and fresh, and filled with Divine energy. You cannot recover an old position by just the old doctrine. You will never recover something of God which has been lost by bringing back the exact statement of the truth. You may be stating the truth of the early days of the New Testament exactly, but you may be far from having the conditions which obtained at such times.

Prophetic succession is not the succession of teaching; it is the succession of anointing. Something can come in from God, by the operation of God; there may be something very real, very living, which God effects through an instrumentality, it may be individual or collective, which is alive because God brought it in under His anointing. And then someone tries to imitate it, duplicate it, or later someone takes it up to carry it on; someone has been appointed, elected, chosen by ballot to be the successor. The thing goes on and grows; but some vital factor is no longer there. The succession is by anointing, not by framework, even of doctrine. We cannot recover New Testament conditions by re-stating New Testament doctrine. We have to get New Testament anointing. I am not dismissing doctrine; it is necessary; but it is the anointing which makes things alive, fresh, vibrant. Everything must come by revelation.

Some of us know what it is to be able to analyse our Bibles and present, perhaps in a very interesting way, the contents of its books and all its doctrines. We can do that with "Ephesians" as well as we can do it with any other book. We can come to "Ephesians" and analyse it and outline the Church and the Body and all that, and be as blind as bats until the day comes when, God having done something in us, something deep and tremendous and terrific, we *see* the Church, we *see* the Body—we *see* "Ephesians"! They were two worlds: one was truth, exact in technical detail, full of interest and fascination—but there was something lacking. We could have stated the truth from beginning to end, but we did not know what was in it; and until we have gone through that experience and something has happened in us, we may think we know, we may be sure we know, we may lay down our life for it; but we do not know. There is all the difference between a very keen, clear, mental apprehension of things in the Word of God, and a spiritual revelation. There is the difference of two worlds—but it is quite impossible to make people understand that difference until something has happened. We shall speak about that 'something that happens' later, but here we are stating the facts. By anointing there is revelation, and revelation by anointing is essential to the seeing of what God is after, both in general and in detail.

So, building up, we arrive at this. A prophetic ministry is that which—although much detail has yet to be revealed, even to the most enlightened servants of God—has, by the Holy Ghost, *seen the purpose of God*, original and ultimate.

(c) EXACT CONFORMITY TO GOD'S THOUGHTS

And then there is the third thing we find connected with this anointing. It is that to which we have already referred in general—*exactness*.

The anointing brings about that *first-hand touch with God*, which means seeing God face to face. Was it not that that was the summing up of Moses' life? "There hath not arisen a prophet since in Israel like unto Moses, whom the Lord knew face to face" (Deut. xxxiv. 10). And when that happens you come into the place of direct spiritual knowledge of God, direct touch with God, the place of the open heaven—you cannot, under any consideration, for any advantage at all, be a person who compromises, who deviates from what has been shown to your heart.

What is it that the Apostle says about Moses? "Moses was faithful in all his house as a servant" (Heb. iii. 5); and the faithfulness of Moses is seen particularly and largely in the way in which he was governed exactly by what God said. You know those later chapters of the book of Exodus, bringing everything back again to the word, again and again and again, "as the Lord commanded Moses." Everything was done as God said; through the whole system which Moses was raised up to constitute and establish, he was exact to a detail. We know why, of course; and here is that great, that grand, comprehensive explanation of what I saw just now about principles. God has Christ in view all the time, in every detail, and that system that Moses instituted was a representation of Christ to a fraction; and so it was necessary that in every detail he should be exact. It is a difficult, costly way, but you cannot have revelation, and go on in revelation, and at the same time compromise over details and have things at any point other than exactly as the Lord wants them. You are not governed by diplomacy or policy or public opinion. You are governed by what the Lord has said in your heart by revelation as to His purpose. That is prophetic ministry.

Prophets were not men who accommodated themselves to anything that was comparative in its goodness. They never let themselves go wholly if the thing was only comparatively good. Look at Jeremiah. There was a day in Jeremiah's life when a good king did seek to recover things, and he did institute a great feast of the Passover, and the people did come up in their crowds for the celebration of that Passover, and it was a great occasion apparently. They were doing great things there in Jerusalem, but with all that was going on which was good, confessedly good, Jeremiah did not let himself go. He had a reservation, and he was right. It was seen afterward that this thing was very largely outward, that the real heart of the people had not changed, the high places were not taken away, and Jeremiah's original prophecy had to stand. If the apparent reformation had been the true thing, then Jeremiah's prophecies about the captivity, the destruction of the city, the complete handing over to judgment, would have gone for nothing. Jeremiah held back. He may not have understood, he may have been in perplexity about it, but his heart would not allow him to go wholly with this comparatively good thing. He found out the reason why afterward—that, although it was good up to a point, it did not represent a deep heart change, and so the judgment had to be.

The prophet cannot accept as full and final what is only comparative, though he rejoices in the measure of good that there may be anywhere. We should, of course, be generous to any little bit of good that is in the world—let us be grateful for anything that is right and true and of God; but oh! we cannot say that is altogether satisfying to the Lord, that is all that the Lord wants. No, this prophetic ministry is one of utter faithfulness to the thoughts of God. It is a ministry of exactness. That is what the anointing means, and we have said why—it is a *full* Christ who is in view.

That last statement in Revelation xix. 10 sums it all up. It gathers up into one sentence prophetic ministry from the beginning. I suppose prophetic ministry commenced in the day when it was stated of the seed of the woman that it should bruise the head of the serpent, and then passed on to Enoch, who prophesied saying, "Behold, the Lord came..." (Jude 14), and so right on from then. It is all gathered up at the end of the Revelation in this thought, that "the testimony of Jesus is the spirit of prophecy." That is, the spirit of prophecy from beginning to end is all toward that—the testimony of Jesus. The spirit of prophecy has always had Him in view from its first utterance—"the seed of the woman"—to "Behold, the Lord came" (and how beginning and end are brought together so early on!). All the way through it was always with the Lord Jesus in view, and a full Christ. "He gave...prophets...till we all attain unto...the fulness of Christ." That is the end, and God can never be satisfied with anything less than the fulness of His Son as represented by the Church. The Church is to be the fulness of Him; a full-grown Man—that is the Church. The prophetic ministry is unto that—the fulness of Christ, the finality of Christ, the all-inclusiveness of Christ. It is to be Christ, centre and circumference; Christ, first and last; Christ in general and Christ in every detail. And to see Christ by revelation means that you can never accept anything less or other. You have seen, and that has settled it. The way to reach God's end, then, is seeing by the Holy Spirit, and that seeing is the basis of this prophetic ministry.

I think that that perhaps is enough to show what I said earlier, that if we see the nature of the ministry, we at once see what the vessel is. The vessel may be individuals fulfilling such a ministry, or it may be collective. Later we may say something more about the vessel, but let us not now think technically, in terms of apostles and prophets and so on, as offices. Let us think of them as vital *functions*. God is concerned that the man and the function are identical, not the man and a professional or official position with a title, whatever the title may be. The vessel must be *that*, and *that* must justify the vessel. We will not go about advertising ourselves as prophets; but God grant that there may be raised up a prophetic ministry for a time like this, when His whole purpose concerning His Son is brought back into view amongst His people. That is their need, and it is His.

TWO

THE MAKING OF A PROPHET

PROPHETIC MINISTRY is something which has not come in with time, but is eternal. It has come out of the eternal counsels.

Perhaps you wonder what that means. Well, we remember that, without any explanation or definition, something comes in right at the beginning and takes the place of government in the economy of God, and involves this very function. When Adam sinned and was expelled from the garden, the Word simply says, God "placed at the east of the garden of Eden the Cherubim...to keep the way of the tree of life" (Genesis iii. 24).

Who or what are the Cherubim? Where do they come from? We have heard nothing about them before; no explanation of them is given. It simply is a statement. God put them there to guard the way of the tree of life. They have become the custodians of life, to hold things according to God's thought. For the thoughts of man's heart have departed from God's thoughts and have become evil; everything has been marred; and now the custodians of the Divine thought about the greatness of all things for man—Divine life, uncreated life—the custodians of that, the Cherubim, are placed there.

But later we are given to understand what the Cherubim are like: this symbolic, composite representation has a four-fold aspect—the lion, the ox, the man and the eagle; and we are given to understand very clearly that the predominate feature is the man. It is a *man*, really, with three other aspects, those of the lion, the ox, and the eagle. The lion is a symbol of kingship or dominion; the ox, of service and sacrifice; the eagle, of heavenly glory and mystery. The man, the predominant aspect of the Cherubim—what is that?

We know that throughout the Scriptures the man takes the place, in the Divine order of things, of the prophet, the representative of God. The representation of God's thoughts is a *man*. That was the intention in the creation of Adam in the image and likeness of God—to be the personal embodiment and expression of all God's thoughts. That is what man was created for. That is what we find in *the* Man, the Man who was God manifested in the flesh. He was the perfect expression of all God's thoughts.

Where has this symbolism of the Cherubim come from? It is simply brought in. It comes out from eternity. It is a Divine, an eternal thought, and it takes charge of things, to hold things for God. So that man—and we know that phrase "the Son of man"—is peculiarly related to the prophetic office, and the prophetic function is an eternal thing, which just comes in. It is, in its very nature, the representation of Divine thoughts, and it is to hold God's thoughts in purity and in fulness. That is the idea related to the man, to the prophet, and that is the prophetic function and nature.

THE IDENTITY OF THE PROPHET
WITH HIS MESSAGE

But what does that carry with it? Here we come to the most important point of the whole. It is the absolute identity of the vessel with the vessel's ministry. Prophetic ministry is not something that you can take up. It is something that you *are*. No academy can make you a prophet. Samuel instituted the schools of the prophets. They were for two purposes—one, the dissemination of religious knowledge, and the other, the writing up of the chronicles of religious history. In Samuel's day there was no open vision; the people had lost the Word of God. They had to be taught the Word of God again, and the chronicles of the ways of God had to be written up and put on record for future generations, and the schools of the prophets were instituted in the main for that purpose. But there is a great deal of difference between those academic prophets and the living, anointed prophets. The academic prophets became members of a profession and swiftly degenerated into something unworthy. All of the false prophets came from schools of prophets, and were accepted publicly on that ground. They had been to college and were accepted. But they were false prophets. Going to a religious college does not of itself make you a prophet of God.

My point is this—the identity of the vessel with its ministry is the very heart of Divine thought. A man is called to represent the thoughts of God, to represent them in what he *is*, not in something that he takes up as a form or line of ministry, not in something that he does. The vessel itself is the ministry and you cannot divide between the two.

THE NECESSITY FOR SELF-EMPTYING

That explains everything in the life of the great prophets. It explains the life of Moses, the prophet whom the Lord God raised up from among his brethren (Deut. xviii. 15, 18). Moses essayed to take up his life-work. He was a man of tremendous abilities, "learned in all the wisdom of the Egyptians" (Acts vii. 22), with great natural qualifications and gifts, and then somehow he got some conception of a life-work for God. It was quite true; it was a true conception, a right idea; he was very honest, there was no question at all about his motives; but he essayed to take up that work on the basis of what he was naturally, with his own ability, qualifications and zeal, and on that basis disaster was allowed to come upon the whole thing.

Not so are prophets made; not so can the prophetic office be exercised. Moses must go into the wilderness and for forty years be emptied out, until there is nothing left of all that as a basis upon which he can have confidence to do the work of God or fulfil any Divine commission. He was by nature a man "mighty in his words and works"; and yet now he says, "I am not eloquent... I am slow of speech..." (Exodus ix. 10). There has been a tremendous undercutting of all natural facility and resource, and I do not think that Moses was merely disagreeable in his reply to God. He did not say in effect, 'You would not allow me to do it then, so I will not do it now.' I think he was a man who was under the Divine discipline and yet on top of it. A man who is really under things and who has become petulant does not respond to little opportunities of helping people. We get a glimpse of Moses at the beginning of his time in the wilderness (Exodus ii. 16, 17) which suggests that he was not of that kind. When there was difficulty at the well, over the watering of the flocks, if Moses had been in a bad mood, cantankerous, disagreeable because the Lord had not seemed to stand by him in Egypt, he probably would have sat somewhere apart and looked on and done nothing to help. But he went readily to help, in a good spirit, doing all he could. He was on top of his trial. Little things indicate where a man is.

We go through times of trial and test under the hand of God, and it is so easy to get into that frame of mind which says in effect, 'The Lord does not want us, He need not have us!' We let everything go, we do not care about anything; we have gone down under our trials and we are rendered useless. I do not believe the Lord ever comes to a person like that to take them up. Elijah, dispirited, fled to the wilderness, and to a cave in the mountains; but he had to get somewhere else before the Lord could do anything with him. "What doest thou *here*, Elijah?" (I Kings xix. 9). The Lord never comes to a man and recommissions him when he is in despair. 'God shall forgive thee all but thy despair' (F.W.H. Myers, *St.*

Paul)—because despair is lost faith in God, and God can never do anything with one who has lost faith.

Moses was emptied to the last drop, and yet he was not angry or disagreeable with God. What was the Lord doing? He was making a prophet. Beforehand, the man would have taken up an office, he would have made the prophetic function serve him, he would have used it. There was no inward, vital relationship between the man and the work that he was to do; they were two separate things; the work was objective to the man. At the end of forty years in the wilderness he is in a state for this to become subjective; something has been done. There has been brought about a state which makes the man fit to be a living expression of the Divine thought. He has been emptied of his own thoughts to make room for God's thoughts; he has been emptied of his own strength, that all the energy should be of God.

Is not that perhaps the meaning of the fire and the bush that was not consumed? It is a parable, maybe a larger parable, but I think in the immediate application it was saying something to Moses. 'Moses, you are a very frail creature, a common bush of the desert, a bit of ordinary humanity, nothing at all of resource in yourself; but there is a resource, which can carry you on and on, and you can be maintained, without being consumed, by an energy that is not your own—the Spirit of God, the energy of God.' That was the great lesson this prophet had to learn. 'I cannot!' 'All right,' says the Lord, 'but I AM.'

A great deal is made of the natural side of many of the Lord's servants, and usually with tragic results. A lot is made of Paul. 'What a great man Paul was naturally, what intellect he had, what training, what tremendous abilities!' That may all be true, but ask Paul what value it was to him when he was right up against a spiritual situation. He will cry, "Who is sufficient for these things?...Our sufficiency is from God" (II Cor. ii. 16; iii. 5). Paul was taken through experiences where he, like Moses, despaired of life. He said, "We... had the sentence of death within ourselves, that we should not trust in ourselves, but in God which raiseth the dead" (II Cor. i. 9).

A MESSAGE INWROUGHT
BY ACTUAL EXPERIENCE

You see, the principle is at work all the time, that God is going to make the ministry and the minister identical. You see it in all the prophets. The Lord stood at nothing. He took infinite pains. He worked even through domestic life, the closest relationships of life. Think of the tragedy of Hosea's domestic life. Think of Ezekiel, whose wife the Lord took away in death at a stroke. The Lord said, "Get up in the morning, anoint your face, allow not the slightest suggestion of mourning or tragedy to be detected; go out as always before, as though nothing had happened; show yourself to the people, go about with a bright countenance, provoke them to enquire what you mean by such outrageous behavior." The Lord brought this heartbreak upon him and then required him to act thus. Why? Ezekiel was a prophet; he had got to embody his message, and the message was this: 'Israel, God's wife, has become lost to God, dead to God, and Israel takes no notice of it; she goes on the same as ever, as though nothing had happened.' The prophet must bring it home by his own experience. God is working the thing right in. He works it in in deep and terrible ways in the life of His servant to produce ministry.

God is not allowing us to take up things and subjects. If we are under the Holy Ghost, He is going to make us prophets; that is, He is going to make the prophecy a thing that has taken place in us, so that what we say is only making vocal something that has been going on, that has been done in us. God has been doing it through years in strange, deep, terrible ways in some lives, standing at nothing, touching everything; and the vessel thus wrought upon, is the message. People do not come to *hear* what you have to *teach*. They have come to *see* what you *are*, to see that thing which has been wrought by God. What a price the prophetic instrument has to pay!

So Moses went into the wilderness, to the awful undoing of his natural life, his natural mentality; to be brought to zero; to have the thing wrought in him. And was God justified?—for after all it was a question of resource for the future. Oh, the strain that was going to bear down upon that life! Sometimes Moses well-nigh broke; at times he did crack under the strain. "I am not able to bear all this people alone, because it is too heavy for me" (Num. xi. 14). What was his resource? Oh, if it had been the old resource of Egypt he would not have stood it for a year. He could not stand provocation in Egypt, he must rise up and fight. He broke down morally and spiritually under that little strain away back there forty years before. What would he do with these rebels? How long would he put up with them? A terrific strain was going to bear down upon him, and only a deep inwrought thing, something that had been done inside, would be enough to carry through when it was a case of standing against the stream for God's full thought.

With us, too, the strain may be terrific; oft-times there will come the very strong temptation—'Let go a little, compromise a little, do not be so utter; you will get more open doors if you will only broaden out a bit; you can have a lot more if you ease up!' What is going to save you in that hour of temptation? The only thing is that God has done this thing in you. It is part of your very being, not something you can give up; it is you, your very life. That is the only thing. God knew what He was doing with Moses. The thing had got to be so much one with the man that there was no dividing between them. The man *was* the prophetic ministry.

He was rejected by his brethren; they would not have him. "Who made thee a prince and a judge over us?" (Ex. ii. 14). That is the human side of it. But there was the Divine side. It was of God that he went into the wilderness for forty years. It had to be, from God's side. It looked as though it was man's doing. But it was not so. These two things went together. Rejection by his brethren was all in line with the sovereign purpose of God. It was the only way in which God got the opportunity He needed to reconstitute this man. The real preparation of this prophet took place during the time that his brethren repudiated him. Oh, the sovereignty of God, the wonderful sovereignty of God! A dark time, a deep time; a breaking, crushing, grinding time; emptied out. It seems as if everything is going, that nothing will be left. Yet all that is God's way of making prophetic ministry.

A MESSENGER DIVINELY ATTESTED

I expect that Moses at the beginning would have been legalistic, laying down the law—'You must do this and that'—and so on; an autocrat or despot. When, after those years, we find him coming off the wheel, out of the hands of the Potter, he is said to be "very meek, above all the men that were upon the face of the earth" (Num. xii. 3), and God could stand by him then. He could not stand by him on that day when he rose up in a spirit of pride, arrogance, self-assertiveness. God had to let that work itself out to its inevitable consequence. But when Moses, as the meekest of men, the broken, humble, selfless man, was challenged by others as to his office—at such a time Moses did not stand up for his position, his rights; he just handed the matter over to the Lord. His attitude was, 'We will allow the Lord to decide. I have no personal position to preserve: if the Lord has made me His prophet, let Him show it. I am prepared to go out of office if it is not of the Lord.' What a different spirit! And the Lord did stand by him marvellously and mightily on those occasions, and terribly so for those who opposed themselves (Numbers xii. 2ff; xvi. 3ff).

PROPHETIC MINISTRY A LIFE, NOT TEACHING

Well, what is a prophet? What is the prophetic function? It is this. God takes hold of a vessel (it may be individual or it may be collective: the function of prophetic ministry may move through a people, as it did through Israel), and He takes that vessel through a deep history, breaking and undoing, disillusioning, revolutionising the whole mentality, so that things which were held fiercely, assertively, are no longer so held. There is developed a wonderful pliableness, adjustableness, teachableness. Everything that was merely objective as to the work of God, as to Divine truth, as to orthodoxy or fundamentalism; all that was held so strongly, in an objective, legalistic way, as to what is right and wrong in methods—it is all dealt with, all broken. There is a new conception entirely, a new outlook upon things; no longer a formal system, something outside you which you take up, but something wrought in an inward way in the vessel. It is what the vessel is that is its ministry. It is not what it has accepted of doctrine and is now teaching.

Oh, to get free of all that horrible realm of things! It is a wretched realm, that of adopting teachings, taking on interpretations, being known because such and such is your line of things. Oh, God deliver us! Oh, to be brought to the place where it is a matter of *life*—of what God has really done in us, made of us! First He has pulverised us, and then He has reconstructed us on a new spiritual principle, and that expresses itself in ministry: what is said is coming from what has been going on behind, perhaps for years and even right up to date.

Do you see the law of prophetic function? It is that God keeps anointed vessels abreast of truth by experience. Every bit of truth that they give out in word is something that has had a history. They went down into the depths and they were saved by that truth. It was their life and therefore it is a part of them. That is the nature of prophetic ministry.

A PROPHET, TOLERANT
BUT UNCOMPROMISING

Reverting to what I was saying about the change in Moses: you can see a reflection of it in the case of Samuel. I think Samuel is one of the most beautiful and loveable characters in the Old Testament, and he is called a prophet. Do you notice that although his own heart is utterly devoted to God's highest and fullest thought, and inwardly he has no compromise whatever, yet he shows a marvellous charity toward Saul during those early months? (It seems not to have gone much beyond a year, the first year of Saul's reign, during which it seems that Saul really did seek to show some semblance of good.) And yet you must remember that Saul represents the denial of the highest of all things—the direct and immediate government of God. Such government was repudiated by Israel in favour of a king—"Make us a king to judge us like all the nations," they said. God said to Samuel: "They have not rejected thee, but they have rejected me" (1 Samuel viii. 5-7).

Kingship was a Divine principle as much as prophecy was. The lion is there with the man. The monarch, representing God's thought of dominion, is there. But with Saul it is on a lower level. His coming in represented the bringing down of that Divine thought to the level of the world: "like all the nations"—a Divine thought taken hold of by carnal men, dragged down to the world level; and Samuel knew it. In his heart he could not accept that and he complained to God about it; he was against this thing, for he saw what it meant. But how charitable he was to Saul as long as he could be!

Why do I say that? Because there is a condition like that existing today. Divine things have been taken hold of by men carnally, and brought

– 21 –

down to an earth level; the direct government of the Holy Spirit has been exchanged for committees and boards and so on. Men have set up the government in Divine things and are running things for God. The way of the New Testament, that in prayer and fasting the mind of the Lord is secured, is hardly known. Well, those who are spiritual, who know, who see, who understand, cannot accept that. But they must be very charitable. A true prophet, like Samuel, will be charitable as long as possible, until that wrong thing takes the pronounced and positive form of disobedience to light given. The Lord came to Saul through Samuel and gave him clearly to understand what he had to do. It was made known to him with unmistakable clearness what God required of him, and he was disobedient. Then Samuel said, 'No more charity with that!' He was implacable. "Because thou hast rejected the word of the Lord, He hath also rejected thee from being king" (I Samuel xv. 23). Samuel went as far as he could while the man did the best he could. That is charity.

Of course, types are always weak and imperfect, but you can see the truth there. The prophet Samuel showed a great deal of forbearance with things that were wrong, even while in his heart he could not accept them. He hoped that light would break and obedience follow and the situation be saved. We have to be very charitable to all that with which we do not agree.

The point is this—Moses had to learn that; he had to be made like that. We are better fitted to serve the Lord's purpose, we are truer prophets, when we can bear with things with which we do not agree, than when in our zeal we are iconoclasts, and seek only to destroy the offending thing. The Lord says, 'That will not do.'

In all that we have said we have emphasized only one thing—that prophetic ministry is a function. Its function is to hold everything in relation to God's full thought—but not as holding a 'line' of things, in an objective and legalistic way. You do not take something up. You can only do it truly as God has wrought into you that thing for which you are going to stand, and in so far as it has been revealed in you through experience, through the handling of God—God has taken you through it, and you know it like that. It is not that you have achieved something, but rather that you have been broken in the process. Now you are fit for something in the Lord.

THREE

A VOICE WHICH MAY BE MISSED

"For they that dwell in Jerusalem, and their rulers, because they knew him not, nor the voices of the prophets which are read every sabbath, fulfilled them by condemning him" (Acts xiii. 27).

THE ABOVE STATEMENT as a whole carries a significance which embraces a very great deal of history, but its direct and immediate implication is that if the people referred to—the dwellers in Jerusalem and their rulers—had been in the good of the most familiar things, they would have behaved very differently from the way in which they did behave. Every week, Sabbath by Sabbath, extending over a very great number of years, they heard things read; but eventually, because of their failure to recognise what they were hearing, they acted in a way entirely opposed to those very things, though under the sovereignty of God fulfilling them in so doing.

Surely that is a word of warning. It represents a very terrible possibility—to hear repeatedly the same things, and not to recognise their significance; to behave in a way quite contrary to our own interests, making for our own undoing, when it might have been otherwise.

The point is this—that there is a voice in the prophets which may be missed, a meaning which may not be apprehended, and the results may be disastrous for the people concerned. "The voices of the prophets": that suggests that there is something beyond the mere things that the prophet says. There is a 'voice.' We may hear a sound, we may hear the words, and yet not hear the voice; that is something extra to the thing said. That is the statement here, that week by week, month after month, and year after year, men read the prophets audibly, and the people who heard the reading did not hear the voices. It is the *voice* of the prophets that we need to hear.

As you go through this thirteenth chapter of the Acts you are able to recognise that this little fragment is in a very crucial context. This chapter, to begin with, marks a development. There in Antioch were certain men, including Saul, and the Holy Ghost said: "Separate me Barnabas and Saul for the work whereunto I have called them." That was a new development, a moving out, something far-reaching, very momentous; but you are not through the chapter before you come upon another crisis, which became inevitable when in a certain place a great crowd came together, and the Jews, refusing to be obedient to the Word, stirred up a revolt. The Apostles made this pronouncement: "It was necessary that the word of God should first be spoken to you. Seeing ye

> **Big things hang upon hearing the voice.**

thrust it from you, and judge yourselves unworthy of eternal life, lo, we turn to the Gentiles" (vs. 46); and they quoted a prophet (Isaiah xlix. 6) for their authority: "I have set thee for a light of the Gentiles." These were epochs in the history of the Church; and the Jews, as a whole, were turned from, and the Gentiles in a very deliberate way were recognised and brought in, because of this very thing—that the Jews had heard these prophets Sabbath by Sabbath but had not heard their voices.

Big things hang upon hearing the voice. Failure to hear may lead to irreparable loss. Very big things concerning Israel have come into the centuries since the time of Acts xiii. It is not my intention to launch out on matters of prophecy concerning the Jews, but my point is this. On the one hand, it was no small thing to fail to hear the voices of the prophets. On the other hand, you notice that the Gentiles rejoiced. It says here, "As the Gentiles heard this, they were glad, and glorified the word of God." Well, on both sides, it is a great thing to fail to hear what could be heard if there were an ear for hearing, and it is a great thing to hear and give heed. I think that is a sufficiently serious foundation and background to engage our attention.

OLD TESTAMENT PROPHETS IN THE NEW TESTAMENT

Let us now look more closely at this matter of "the voices of the prophets." A fact of very great significance is this, that the prophets have such a large place in the New Testament. I wonder if you have taken account of how large that place is. You will not need to be reminded of how largely the Gospels call upon the major prophets, as they are called. "That it might be fulfilled which was spoken by the prophet..."—how often that statement alone occurs in the Gospels. It came in from the birth of the Lord Jesus, and in that connection alone on several occasions the major prophets are quoted. But when you move from the Gospels into the Acts and the Epistles, you move largely into what are called the minor prophets—not minor because they were of less account than the others, but because the record of their writings is smaller. It is tremendously impressive and significant that these minor prophets should be drawn upon so extensively in the New Testament; they are quoted over fifty times.

PROPHETS MEN OF VISION

From that general significance, two factors emerge. One as to the prophets themselves; why do they have so large a place in the New Testament? Well, the answer to that will be largely another question. What do prophets signify? They are the 'seers' (I Samuel ix. 9); they are the men who see and, in seeing, act as eyes for the people of God. They are the men of vision; and their large place in the New Testament surely therefore indicates how tremendously important spiritual vision is for the people of God throughout this dispensation. Of course, the other thing is the vision itself, but I am not concerned just now to speak about what the vision was and is—that, with other aspects, may come later. At the moment, I feel the Lord is concerned with this factor—the tremendous importance of spiritual vision if the people of God are to fulfil their vocation. It resolves itself into a matter solely of vision unto vocation, and the vocation will not be fulfilled without vision.

VISION IMPARTS PURPOSE TO LIFE

So for a moment let us dwell upon the place of vision—and you will not think that I am talking about 'visionariness.' No, it is something specific, it is *the* vision, it is something clearly defined. The prophets knew what they were talking about—not merely abstract ideas, but something very definite. Vision is something quite specific, something with which the Lord is concerned and which has become a mighty, dominating thing in the life of those who have it; clear, distinct, precise, specific; taking hold of and mastering and dominating them, so that the whole purpose of existence itself is gathered into it. Such people are at the place where they know why they have an existence, they know the purpose for which they are alive and are able to say what it is, and their horizon is bounded by that thing; they, with their whole life in all its aspects, are gathered into that, poised to that. It is an object which governs everything for them. It is not just living on this earth and doing many things and getting through somehow; but everything that has a place in life is linked with this definite, distinct, all-governing objective. It is such a vision which gives meaning to life.

It is not necessary for me to take you through Israel's history as governed by that very truth. You know quite well that, when Israel was in a right position, that is how things were—focused, definite, with everybody centred in one object. And, before we go further, let us say again that all these prophets—men who were the eyes of God for a people, and signifying to that people God's thought and purpose concerning them, their Divine vocation, God's interpretation of their very existence—these prophets who embodied that are all brought into the New Testament dispensation and into the Church, with this clear implication, that that is how the Church is to be if it is to get through. The Church is to be a *seeing* thing, dominated by a specific object and vision, knowing why it exists, having no doubt about it, and poised in utter abandonment thereto, bringing all other things in life into line with that. Our attitude has to be that, while in this world we necessarily have to do this and that, to earn our living and do our daily work, yet there is something governing all else: there is a Divine vision. These things have to blend to that one Divine end.

That is the first implication of the fact that the prophets have such a large place in this dispensation. We cannot now stay to follow that out in detail from the Word, but it would be very helpful to go through the New Testament, and see how the bringing in of the prophets is made to apply to the varied aspects of the Church's life. It is very impressive.

VISION A UNIFYING FACTOR

The prophets are governing this dispensation in this way. This vision, *the* vision, was the very cohesiveness and strength of Israel. When the vision was clearly before them, when their eyes were opened and they were seeing, when they were in line with God's purpose, when they were governed by that end to which God had called them, they were one people, made one by the vision. They had a single eye. That little phrase, "If...thine eye be single..." (Matthew vi. 22), has a great deal more in it than we have recognised. A single eye—it unifies the whole life and conduct; it will unify all your behaviour. If you are a man or a woman of one idea, everything will be brought into that. Of course, that is not always a very happy thing, though in this case it is. People who are obsessed and, as we say, 'have a bee in their bonnet,' with nothing else to talk about but one thing, are often very trying people. But there is a right way, a Divine way, in which the people of God should be people of a single eye, a single idea; and that singleness of eye brings all the faculties into coordination.

During the rare periods when Israel was like that, they were a marvellously unified people. On the other hand, you can see how, when the vision faded and failed, they disintegrated, became people of all kinds of divided and schismatic interests and activities, quarrelling amongst themselves. How true is the word: "Where there is no vision, the people perish (go to pieces)" (Proverbs xxix. 18). And so it was with Israel. See them in the days of Eli, when there was no open vision. What a disintegrated, disunited people they were! That happened many times. The vision was a solidifying, cohesive power, making a people solidly one, and in that oneness was their strength, and they were irresistible. See them over Jordan in their assault upon Jericho! See them moving triumphantly on! While they were governed by one object, none could stand before them. Their strength was in their unity, and their unity was in their vision. The enemy knows what he is doing in destroying or confusing vision: he is dividing the people of God.

VISION A DEFENSIVE POWER

What a defensive power is vision like that! What little chance the enemy has when we are a people set upon one thing! If we have all sorts of divided and personal interests, the enemy can make awful havoc. He does not get a chance when everybody is centred upon one Divine object. He has to divide us somehow, distract us, disintegrate us, before he can accomplish his work of hindering God's end. All those features of self-pity, self-interest, which are ever seeking to get in and spoil, will never get in while vision is clear and we are focused upon it as one people. It is tremendously defensive. The Apostle spoke about being "in diligence not slothful; fervent in spirit; serving the Lord" (Romans xii. 11). Moffatt translates "fervent in spirit" as "maintaining the spiritual glow." Being centred upon an object wholeheartedly is a wonderfully protective thing. Such a condition in a people closes the breaches and resists the encroachments and impingements of all kinds of things which would distract and paralyse.

VISION MAKES FOR DEFINITENESS AND GROWTH

Vision was like a flame with the prophets. You have to recognise that about them, at any rate—that these men were flames of fire. There was nothing neutral about them; they were aggressive, never passive. Vision has that effect. If you have really seen what the Lord is after, you cannot be half-hearted. You cannot be passive if you see. Find the person who has seen, and you find a positive life. Find the person who does not see, is not sure, is not clear, and you find a neutral, a negative, one that does not count. These prophets were men like flames of fire because they saw. And when Israel was in the good of the Divine calling, Israel was like that—positive, aggressive. When the vision faded, they came to a standstill, turned in upon themselves, went round and round in circles, ceased to get anywhere.

This aggressiveness, this positiveness, which is the fruit of having seen, provides the Lord with the ground that He needs for a right kind of training and discipline. It does not mean that we shall never make mistakes. You will see in the New Testament—and I hope you will not charge me with heresy—that even a man as crucified as Paul could make mistakes. Peter, a man so used and so chastened, could make mistakes. Yes, apostles could make mistakes. And prophets could make mistakes. "What doest thou here Elijah?" (I Kings xix. 9). 'You have no business to be here'—that is what it means. Yes, prophets and apostles could make mistakes, and they did; but there is this about it—because they had seen, and were utterly abandoned to that which they had seen of the Lord's mind, the Lord was abundantly able to come in on their mistakes and sovereignly overrule them and teach His servants something more of Himself and His ways.

Now, you never find that with people who are indefinite. The indefinite people, those who are not meaning business, who are not abandoned, never do learn anything of the Lord. It is the people who commit themselves, who let go and go right out in the direction of whatever measure of light the Lord has given them, who, on the one hand, find their mistakes—the mistakes of their very zeal—taken hold of by Divine sovereignty and overruled; and, on the other hand, are taught by the Lord through their very mistakes what His thoughts are, how He does things, and how He does not do them. If we are going to wait in indefiniteness and uncertainty and do nothing until we know it all, we shall learn nothing.

Have you not noticed that it is the men and women whose hearts are aflame for God, who have seen something truly from the Lord and have been mightily gripped by what they have seen, who are the people that are learning? The Lord is teaching them; He does not allow their blunders and their mistakes to engulf them in destruction. He sovereignly overrules, and in the long run they are able to say, 'Well, I made some awful blunders, but the Lord marvellously took hold of them and turned them to good account.' To be like this, with vision which gathers up our whole being and masters us, provides the Lord with the ground for looking after us even when we make mistakes—because His interests are at stake, His interests and not our own are the concern of our heart. The prophets and the apostles learned to know the Lord in wonderful ways by their very mistakes, for they were the mistakes, not of their own stubborn self-will, but of a real passion for God and for what He had shown them as to His purpose.

VISION GIVES ASCENDENCY TO GOD'S PEOPLE

And then note that the very ascendency of Israel was based upon vision. They were called of God to be an ascendent people, above all the peoples of the earth, set in the midst of the nations as a spiritually governmental vessel. The Lord did promise that no nation should be able to take headship over them. His thought for them was that they should be "the head, and not the tail" (Deut. xxviii. 13). But that was not going to happen willy-nilly, irrespective of their condition and position. It was when they had the vision before them clearly, corporately, as an entire people—dominated, mastered, unified by the vision—it was then that they were head and not tail, it was then that they were in the ascendent.

And that brings in these prophets again. (We think now of the later prophets of Israel.) Why the prophets? Because Israel had lost their position. Assyria, Babylon and the rest were taking ascendency over them because they had lost their vision. It is in the minor prophets, as they are called, that you have so much about this very matter. "My people are destroyed for lack of knowledge" (Hosea iv. 6). That is a note to which all the prophets are tuned. Why this state of things? Why is Israel now the underdog of the nations? The answer is—lost vision. The prophet comes to try to get them back to the place of the vision. The prophet has the vision, he is the eyes of the people: he is calling them back to that for which God chose them, to show them anew why He took them from among the nations.

VISION NEEDED BY EVERY CHILD OF GOD

All this is but an emphasis upon the place of vision. It may not get you very far; you may wonder what it all leads to. You are saying now, 'Well, what is the vision?' That is not the point at the moment; that can come later. The point is that that is the necessity, the absolute necessity for the Church to-day—for you, for me; and let me say at once that, while it is pre-eminently a corporate thing—that is, it is something which is to be in a people, even though that people be but a remnant, a small number amongst all the people of God—while pre-eminently a corporate thing, it must also be personal. You and I individually must be in the place where we can say, 'I have seen, I know what God is after!'

If we were asked why the Church is as it is to-day, in so large a measure of impotence and disintegration, and what is needed to bring about an impact from heaven by means of the Church, could we say? Is it presumption to claim to be able to do that? The prophets knew; and remember that the prophets, whether they were of the Old Testament or of the New Testament, were not an isolated class of people, they were not some body apart, holding this in themselves officially. They were the very eyes of the body. They were, in the thought of God, *the people* of God. You know that principle; it is seen, for instance, in the matter of the High Priest. God looks upon the one High Priest as Israel, and deals with all Israel on the ground of the condition of the High Priest, whether it be good or bad. If the High Priest is bad—"And he showed me Joshua the high priest...clothed with filthy garments" (Zechariah iii. 1-5)—that is Israel. God deals with Israel as one man.

The prophet is the same; and that is why the prophet was so inter-woven with the very condition and life of the people. Listen to the prophet Daniel praying. Personally he was not guilty; personally he had not sinned as the nation had sinned; but he took it all on himself and spoke as though it were his responsibility, as if he were the chief of sin-ners. These men were brought right into it. There is such a oneness between the prophets and the people in condition, in experience, in suf-fering, that they can never view themselves as officials apart from all that, as it were talking to it from the outside; they are in it, they *are* it.

My meaning is this, that we are not to have vision brought to us by a class called ministers, prophets and apostles. They are here only to keep us alive to what we ought to be before God, how we ought to be; con-stantly stirring us up and saying, 'Look here, this is what you ought to be.' It ought therefore to be, with every one of us personally, that we are in the meaning of this prophetic ministry. The Church is called to be a prophet to the nations. May I repeat my enquiry—it is a permissible ques-tion without admitting of any presumption—could you say what is need-ed by the Church to-day? Could you interpret the state of things, and explain truly by what the Lord has shown you in your own heart? I know the peril and dangers that may surround such an idea, but that is the very meaning of our existence. It will be in greater or lesser degree in every one of us, but, either more or less, we have the key to the situation. God needs people of that sort. It must be individual.

VISION CALLS FOR COURAGE

But remember it will call for immense courage. Oh, the courage of these prophets!—courage as over against compromise and policy. Oh, the ruinous effects of policy, of secondary considerations! 'How will it affect our opportunities if we are so definite? Will it not lessen our opportuni-ties of serving the Lord if we take such a position?' That is policy, and it is a ruinous thing. Many a man who has seen something, and has begun to speak about what he has seen, has found such a reaction from his own brethren and amongst those where his responsibility lay, that he has drawn back. 'It is dangerous to pursue that any further.' Policy! No, there was nothing of that about the prophets. Are we committed because we have seen?

There will be cost; we may as well face it. There is a little fragment in Hebrews ix–"They were sawn asunder." A tradition says that that applied to the prophet Isaiah–that he was the one who was sawn asunder. Read Isaiah liii. There is nothing more sublime in all the literature of the Bible, and for that he was sawn asunder. Was he right? Well, we to-day stand on the ground, and in the good, of his rightness. But the devil does not like that, and so Isaiah was sawn asunder. There are tremendous values bound up with seeing, and with uncompromising abandonment to the vision, but there is very great cost also.

We will leave it there for the time being; but we must have dealings with the Lord and say, 'How much have I seen? After all I have heard of the prophets week by week, after all the conventions, the conferences, the meetings I have been attending, have I heard the *voice* of the prophets after all? I have heard the speakers give their messages and addresses: have I heard the voice?' The effect will be far-reaching if we have. If we have not, it is time we got to the Lord about it. This must not go on! What happened in Acts xiii? Hearing they did not hear; but where there was a hearing, oh, what tremendous things happened, what tremendous values came!

FOUR

A VISION THAT CONSTITUTES A VOCATION

"For they that dwell in Jerusalem, and their rulers, because they knew him not, nor the voices of the prophets which are read every sabbath, fulfilled them by condemning him" (Acts xiii. 27).

WE POINTED OUT at the beginning of the previous chapter that the above statement indicates that there is something more to be heard than the audible reading of the Word of God. "The voices of the prophets." What are the prophets saying?—not, what were the actual words used by the prophets, the sentences and statements, the form of their pronouncements, but what did it all amount to *in effect*? These dwellers and rulers in Jerusalem could have quoted the prophets without difficulty; they probably could have recited the contents of all the books of the prophets. They were well-drilled in the content of the Old Testament Scriptures, but they never stopped and asked the simple questions: 'What does it amount to? What really is the implication? What were these men after?' And because they never did that, they never got further than the letter.

VOCATION MISSED BECAUSE VISION LOST

We are asking those questions now. What is that which is within and behind and deeper than the written and spoken utterances of the prophets? We know that the prophets were dealing with a situation which by no means represented the Lord's mind regarding His people. I could make it stronger than that, and say the situation was very far from the Lord's thought; but I have present conditions in mind, rather than any extreme state of things, and so I simply say that the condition did not then, nor does it now, really represent the Lord's mind and intention where His people were and are concerned. The prophets were dealing with such a situation, and, because it was like that, the real vocation of the people of God was not being fulfilled. They were failing in that for which the Lord had really brought them into being. Whereas they ought to have been a people of tremendous spiritual strength in the midst of the nations, with a real impact of God upon the nations, with a note of great authority which had to be taken account of—"Thus saith the Lord," declared in such a way that people really had to heed—whereas it ought to have been like that, they were failing. There was weakness and failure. The prophets sought to get down to the root of that situation, to get behind that deplorable condition and that tragic failure. To get there, of course, they had to work their way through a lot of positive factors in the condition. There were all the things to which the prophets referred—sins and so on; but the prophets were solid as one man on one particular thing, that back of these conditions, resulting in this main failure, the cause was lost vision. The people had lost their original vision, the vision which had at one time been clearly before them.

When God laid His hand upon them and brought them out of Egypt, they had a vision. They saw the purpose and intention of God. It became the exultant note of their song on the farther side of the Red Sea. I am not going to stay for the moment with what that purpose was. But they were a people to whom God had given a vision of His purpose concerning them, both as to themselves and as to their vocation. They had lost it, and this was the result; and the prophets, in dealing with that, lighted solidly upon this one thing: 'Your vocation in its fulness of realisation and accomplishment rests upon your vision, and fulness of vocation requires fulness of vision.' That means that if your vision becomes less than God's fulness, you will only go so far, and then you will stop. If you are going right on and through to all that God meant in constituting you His vessel, you must have fulness of vision; God is never satisfied with anything less than fulness. The very fact that you cannot go any further than your vision leads you is God's way of saying, 'You must have fulness of vision if you are coming to fulness of purpose and realisation.'

Now, that is the very foundation of the thing with which we are occupied just now. The prophets were always speaking about this matter. We previously quoted Hosea iv. 6: "My people are destroyed for lack of knowledge: because thou hast rejected knowledge, I will also reject thee, that thou shalt be no priest to me." That is only saying in other words, 'My people go to pieces for lack of vision; you have closed your eyes to My purpose which I presented to you; I have no further use for you'; and that is a very strong statement. It links with another passage: "Israel is swallowed up: now are they among the nations as a vessel wherein none delighteth" (Hosea viii. 8, A.R.V.).

If you want to get the full force of that, look at a word in Jeremiah's prophecies. "Is this man Coniah a despised broken vessel? Is he a vessel wherein none delighteth? Wherefore are they cast out, he and his seed, and are cast into the land which they know not? O earth, earth, earth, hear the word of the Lord. Thus saith the Lord, Write ye this man childless, a man that shall not prosper in his days; for no more shall a man of his seed prosper, sitting upon the throne of David, and ruling in Judah" (Jer. xxii. 28-30, A.R.V.). "Israel...among the nations as a vessel wherein none delighteth." "Coniah...a vessel wherein none delighteth...Write ye this man childless." There is no future for a vessel like that. We might well say of Israel as of Coniah, "Write this man childless." That is an end. A continuation, going right through without that arrest, demands fulness of vision.

VISION, NOT KNOWLEDGE OF FACTS, QUALIFIES FOR VOCATION

Do give heed to this, especially my younger brothers and sisters in Christ. The fulfillment of that into which you are called through the grace of God—what you may call the service of God, the work of the Lord; what we will sum up as Divine vocation—*must* rest upon a vision which the Lord has given you: a vision, of course, that is not just something in itself but is *the* vision which He has given concerning His Church. You must have that. Then the measure in which you will go right on and through to fulness will be the measure of your vision—the measure in which you have come personally to possess that Divine vision. There can be all sorts of things less than that which lead you into Christian work. You may hear an appeal for workers, an appeal for missionaries, an appeal to service based upon some Scripture—"Go ye into all the world, and preach the gospel"—and so on. And with the accompaniments of that appeal you may be moved, stirred up, feel very solemn; something may happen in the realm of your emotions, your feelings, your reason, and you may take that as a Divine call. Now, I am not saying that no one has ever served the Lord properly and truly on that basis: do not misunderstand me: but I do want to say there can be all that, and in a very intense form, and yet it can be not your own but someone else's vision which has been passed over to you, and that will not do.

'But,' you say, 'there is the Scripture—"Go ye into all the world, and preach the gospel."' Remember, those to whom those words were addressed had all the facts about Christ—the incarnation, the virgin birth, His life, His teaching, His miracles, His Cross, and all the accompanying heavenly attestations. Some of those very men—John's disciples—were there when the voice from heaven said, "This is my beloved Son." Others were on the mountain when again the voice said, "This is my beloved Son." They saw the transfiguration, and they saw Him in resurrection. Is that not enough with which to go out to the world—all that mass of

mighty facts? Surely they can go and proclaim what they know? But no—
"Tarry ye in Jerusalem."

What was it eventually that constituted them men who could fulfil
and obey that command to go? 'Well,' you say, 'of course it was the presence of the Holy Spirit.' Perfectly true. But was there not something else?
Why the forty days after His resurrection? Do you not think that they
were getting through the externals, the events, and *seeing* something—
seeing what no human eye could see, what could never be seen by any
amount of objective demonstration? If the Apostle Paul is anything to go
by in this matter, he will tell us perfectly plainly that his whole life and
ministry and commission were based upon one thing: "It was the good
pleasure of God...to reveal His Son in me, that I might preach Him among
the Gentiles." "I make known to you, brethren, as touching the gospel
which was preached by me, that it is not after man. For neither did I
receive it from man, nor was I taught it, but it came to me through revelation of Jesus Christ." (Galatians i. 15, 16; 11, 12.)

All the other things may be facts which we possess by reading our
New Testament. We have it all and we may believe it as the substance of
Christianity. That does not constitute us missionaries to go out and proclaim the facts of Christ—facts though they be. That is not it. How many
have done so! How far have they gone? They go so far and then stop. We
cannot stay to dwell upon the limitation. Dear friends, there is terrible
limitation in the Church just now, limitation of the knowledge of the
Lord, even on the part of many who have been the Lord's servants for a
long period of years. There are many Christians, even of years' standing,
to whom it is actually difficult to talk about the things of the Lord.

THE VISION—GOD'S FULL PURPOSE IN REDEMPTION

But reverting to Israel: you do not find anything concerning Israel
that suggests or indicates that they came out of Egypt, and were in the
wilderness and later in the land, to declare as their gospel that God
brought them out of the land of Egypt. That was not their message. Of
course, it is recounted many times, but that was not their message, not
what they were proclaiming. What was it that was always in their view?

It was what they were brought out for. It was God's vision in bringing them out. So many of us have settled down to preach just the 'coming out' side—salvation from sin, from the world. It goes just so far, but the Church does not get very far with that. It is good, it is right, of course; it is a part of the whole; but it is only a part. It is the full vision that is needed to go right through. Oh, the pathos associated with the lives of many of the Lord's servants! They come to a standstill, in a realm of limited life and power and influence, because their vision is so small. Is that not true?

What am I saying to you? First of all, if you are going right through, to serve the Lord in any full way, you must have revealed to your own heart God's purpose concerning His Son. You will have to be able to say that God has 'revealed His Son in you,' in this sense, that you see, not merely your own deliverance from sin, but God's purpose concerning His Son unto which you are saved—the big thing, the full thing. You are only a fragment in it. That is the basis of service, of vocation; and these very Apostles were held back until there broke upon them the full blaze of the meaning of Christ risen and ascended—the vision of the glorified Christ and all that that signified in the eternal purpose of God. Then they went out, and we find their message was always, not the gospel of God concerning personal salvation, but "the gospel of God...concerning His Son," Jesus Christ. They had seen, not the historic Jesus, but the glorified Christ of God; and they had not just seen Him as an objective vision, but His true significance had broken in upon them.

What a change it represented from the old days, when they were always thinking in terms of the coming Messiah who would set up a temporal kingdom on this earth, with themselves seated on His right hand and on His left! They would be notable people down here on this earth, and would oust the Romans from their country! That thing on the earth was their full and only vision—fighting with literal arms, revolting against literal usurpers of their country.

But oh, what a vast change when they saw His kingdom! Now, the thing which had held them in its grip simply went, not to be thought of any longer. Seeing His kingdom! He had said, "There are some of them that stand here, who shall in no wise taste of death, till they see the Son of man coming in his kingdom" (Matthew xvi. 28). What is the kingdom? It is Christ, far above all rule and authority, the centre and the goal of all Divine counsels from eternity. That is language, of course—mere words; but the import needs to be apprehended. You must have vision in your own heart before you can be a servant of God who will get very far, and you have to have growing vision in order to get right through. Come back to Hosea. "My people are destroyed for lack of knowledge" (Hosea iv. 6). What does he say a little later? "Let us know, let us follow on to know the Lord" (Hosea vi. 3). It is growing, progressive vision that brings us through to God's full end. It must be like that—not being contented with two or three facts about Christ and salvation, but having the eyes of our hearts enlightened to see Him.

What I am saying, of course, is a statement of facts. I cannot give you anything, I cannot bring you into it; but I can, I trust, influence you a little in the direction of going to the Lord and saying, 'Now, Lord, if Thou needest me, I am available, I am at Thy disposal; but Thou must lay the foundation, and open my eyes, and give me the requisite vision that will mean that I do not only go out and preach things about Christ.' Something very much more than that is needed.

That is the first thing, and it applies to us all, not only to those who are going out into what we call 'full-time service.'

ISRAEL'S VOCATION—TO EXPRESS GOD'S PRESENCE AMONG THE NATIONS

Saying that, I am able to come to the next thing for the moment. What was the vision that Israel had lost and to which the prophets were seeking to bring the people back? The vision was this—the very vocation for which God had laid His hand upon Israel, the meaning of their existence as Israel. What was that?

The movement of God was like this. Here are nations and peoples spreading all over the earth. Out from those nations God takes one solitary individual, Abram, and places him, so to speak, right at the centre of the nations. That is the spiritual geography of it. And then God raises up from that man a seed, and constitutes his seed a nation right in the midst of the nations; distinct from the nations, perfectly distinct, but in the midst. Then God constitutes that nation on heavenly principles—a corporate body constituted on heavenly, Divine, spiritual principles, with God Himself in the midst—with the result that all the other nations gather round to look on.

And what do those nations take account of? Not of the preaching of this nation in their midst; you have nothing about their preaching at all—that is, the proclaiming of doctrines and truths. But the onlookers become aware that God, the only true and living God, is there. There is no mistaking it, they cannot get away from it, they have to recognise it: God is there. Because this people is so constituted, God is there, and there is a registration of God all around, wherever these people come. Ah, even before they come, something is beginning to happen. Listen to Rahab! What did she say to the spies? Israel has not arrived yet, but she says, 'We know all about you. We know what you signify. We have heard all about it.' Already the fear of this people is ahead of them. There is something of spiritual power there which does not have to be preached in words. The people are there, with God in their midst—because God has His heavenly thoughts and principles as the very constitution of their life. He is there; the rest follows.

Now I have gathered into that statement the whole of the Bible, Old and New Testaments. As to the Old Testament, what was Israel's Divine vocation? Not primarily to say things about God, but to be as God in the midst of the nations. "God is in the midst of her; she shall not be moved" (Psalm xlvi. 5). 'The Lord is here!' How much that counted for! That was their vocation. You may say that in the Old Testament it was type; but oh, it was much more than type, it was very real; it was a fact.

THE CHURCH'S VOCATION—TO EXPRESS
THE LORDSHIP OF CHRIST

When we come into the New Testament we find ourselves in the presence of a double development. God is here present in the Person of His Son, Jesus Christ. His name is Emmanuel—'God with us'—and all who

have to do with Him have to do with God in a very personal and immediate way. He claims that His very physical body is the temple of God.

Then, through His death, resurrection, and ascension, He returns in
the Person of the Holy Spirit and takes up His residence in the Church,
which is His Body. Things then begin to happen quite spontaneously, out
from the world of spiritual intelligences—not just because of certain doctrines being preached, but because of that Divine presence.

There are conscious intelligences all around, behind men and
nations, and the conflict has started; not because of what God's people
say, but because they are here. Let that be corporate, and you have God's
idea of vocation. This is not the dispensation of the conversion of the
nations. I wonder even if this is the dispensation of the full evangelization of the nations. We are hoping the Lord may come any day. Half of
this world has never heard the name of Jesus yet, after two thousand
years. If the Lord is coming to-night, something has to happen if the
world is to be evangelized before He comes! That is not said to stay or
weaken evangelization. Let us get on with it and do all that is possible;
but, remember, the Lord has given us His meaning for this dispensation.
"This gospel of the kingdom shall be preached in the whole world *for a
testimony* unto all the nations; and then shall the end come" (Matthew
xxiv. 14).

Look at your New Testament. It was said, "Their sound went out into
all the earth" (Romans x. 18). It was said then that the whole world was
touched. But the world has grown a good deal
since then. What happened at that time? The
Lord planted nuclei, corporate representa-
tions of His Church, first in one nation and
then in another, and by their presence the
fight broke out. The one thing that Satan was
bent upon was to eject that which inoculated
his kingdom with the sovereignty of the Lord;
to get it out, break it up, disintegrate it, somehow to nullify it; turning those concerned one
against another, creating divisions—anything
to spoil, to mar, to destroy their representation

> **God's object is to get into the nations a corporate expression of the lordship of His Son.**

of Christ's absolute lordship; to neutralise that, to get it out, to drive it out, to do anything to get rid of this thing inside his kingdom. Satan's kingdom has acted in this way, as if to say: 'While that thing is here, we can never be sure of ourselves; while that is here our kingdom is divided, it is not whole: let us get it out, in order to have our kingdom solid.'

God's object is to get into the nations a corporate expression of the lordship of His Son—to have His place there. I am not saying we are not to preach; yes, we must preach, witness, testify; but the essential thing is that the Lord must *be* there. There are times—and this will be borne out by many servants of God—when you cannot preach, you cannot do anything but hold on where you are, being there, standing there, keeping in close touch with heaven there. You can do nothing else, and the waves break upon you. It has happened many times. Before ever there has been any advance or development there has been a long-drawn-out period in which the one question has been, 'Shall we be able to hold on, to stand our ground?' Satan has said, 'Not if I can help it! You will go out if I can do anything about it!'

The whole question at issue is the foothold of the heavenly Lord in the nations. Israel was constituted for that; the Church is constituted for that. It cannot be done single-handed by units; it requires the corporate—the two, the three; the more the better, provided there is the unifying factor, the oneness, of a single eye. If double motives and personal interests come in, they will undo it all. Are you fighting a lonely battle? You need co-operation, you need corporate help to fight that battle through and to hold your ground. Mark you, the enemy will drive you out if he can. Preach if you can; but if you cannot, that does not mean that you are to quit. Until the Lord says, 'I can do no more here,' you have to hold on. Do we not know the terrific efforts of the enemy to drive us out? Many of you have gone far enough to know what that means. If he could put you out, he would.

But that is the vision—what the Church is constituted for in relation to the Lord Jesus: so that, in the light of the coming day, you are standing as a testimony of the coming day; in the nations for a testimony, "until he come whose right it is" to reign, and "the kingdom of the world is become the kingdom of our Lord, and of his Christ" (Rev. xi. 15); a foothold unto that time; an altar built, which testifies: 'This belongs to the Lord: the Lord's rights are here: He has purchased this.' But you will find every kind of contradiction to that in conditions, and every kind of assault from the enemy to try to prove that the Lord has not anything there, that He has no footing, and that you had better get out.

Do you see how necessary it is to have the vision? You cannot do that on enthusiasm—it will not last; nor on someone else's vision—it will not support you to the end. You must be like this man Paul and those who "endured, as seeing him who is invisible"; not as having seen Him long ago, but living continually in the light of what you have seen and are seeing, a light which is ever growing.

VISION IS THE MEASURE OF VOCATION

Now, if all this is simple and elementary, it is nevertheless basic. Do you see that vision of God's full purpose concerning His Son, revealed in your own heart in its beginnings, but then growing clearer and fuller, is the basis of vocation? I do trust that nothing I have said will have the effect of making you less earnest and devoted in all simple ways of witnessing, or testifying concerning salvation; but do remember that, for fulness, you need to see very much more than that. You will go just as far as your vision takes you; therefore, we all have need of Paul's prayer that God "may give unto you a spirit of wisdom and revelation in the knowledge of him; having the eyes of your heart enlightened, that ye may know what is the hope of His calling, what the riches of the glory of his inheritance in the saints, and what the exceeding greatness of his power to us-ward who believe" (Ephesians i. 17-19).

That is the vision. And then, as is written in Isaiah xxv. 7 (A.R.V.): "...he will destroy (*lit.* swallow up) in this mountain the face of the covering that covereth all peoples, and the veil that is spread over all nations." What does that mean—"this mountain"? What mountain? Well, it is Zion. But has that literal mountain, Mount Zion, that rocky eminence in Jerusalem, ever been the instrument of taking the covering veil from

off all faces? Of course it has not! What is Zion? Zion, in spiritual interpretation, is that people who are living in the good of the Lord's complete
sovereignty. It says in the immediate context, "He hath swallowed up
death for ever" (vs. 8). It is through His triumph, the triumph of His Cross
and resurrection, that He comes to us. "Ye are come unto mount Zion"
(Hebrews xii. 22). Zion is the realm of His absolute lordship, and a people living in the good of His lordship. Then the veil is taken away. What
the Lord wants here and there and there are these nuclei, these little com-
panies of people living in the good of His victory, living in the good of His
having swallowed up death victoriously; and where they are, people will
see; they will be the instrument for taking the veil from other people's
faces. Where such a company is found, there you see the Lord. When you
come into touch with those people, you come into touch with reality.

So the final appeal is that everything must be adjusted and brought
into line with the vision, and the one question for us is this: Are people
seeing the Lord? It is not a matter of whether they are hearing what we
have to talk about—our preaching, doctrine, interpretation—but: Are they
seeing the Lord, are they feeling the Lord, are they meeting the Lord? Oh,
I do not ask you in your different locations to gather two or three together to study certain kinds of Bible teaching; but I do ask you to ask the
Lord to constitute you corporately that which will have a spiritual impact,
that in which the Lord can be seen, the Lord can be found; of which it
can be said, 'The Lord is there!' May that be true of us, wherever we are.

FIVE

WHY THE PROPHET'S MESSAGE IS NOT APPREHENDED

Reading: Acts xiii. 27, 15; II Corinthians iii. 14-18; Isaiah liii. 1.

THE PROPHETS WERE READ, as Paul points out here, every Sabbath. It was the fixed custom to read the law and the prophets every Sabbath, and it may be pointed out that it was not just at one particular time in the day that this was done, but all through the Sabbath day the law and the prophets were being read in the synagogues. And yet it says that although the very rulers themselves, as well as the dwellers in Jerusalem who attended the temple, heard that reading of the prophets so continuously, they never heard the *voices* of the prophets. And because they failed to hear that inner something, which was more than just the audible reading of what the prophets had said, they lost everything that was intended for them, as this thirteenth chapter of Acts shows. The Apostles left them and turned to the Gentiles, who had an ear ready to hear.

That is a matter of no small consequence and seriousness. It is evident that it behoves *us* to seek to hear the voices of the prophets, really to know what the prophets were saying. Let us again look at the statement: "...because they knew him not, nor the voices of the prophets." Why did they not know? Why did they not hear? This is one basic answer to that enquiry which is going to occupy us just now, and which brings us down to foundations, really to the root of things.

THE OFFENCE OF THE CROSS
(a) A SUFFERING MESSIAH

The answer to that enquiry is this—because they were not willing to accept the Cross. That is what went to the root of the whole matter. Firstly, they were not willing to admit of a suffering Messiah. They had their own minds well made up, both as to what kind of Messiah their Messiah would be, and as to what He would do, and as to the results of His advent; and anything that ran counter to that fixed mentality was not only not accepted—it was an offence. They could not admit into the realm of their contemplation that their coming Messiah would be a suffering Messiah. Yet the prophets were always speaking about the suffering Messiah. Isaiah, at that point in his prophecies which we know as chapter liii, presents the classic on the suffering Messiah, and yet he opens by saying: "Who hath believed our message?"

I think we need not stay to gather further evidence that that was their attitude. Right the way through it was just that. Paul, in his letter to the Galatians, was dealing with that very thing. Towards the end of the letter he spoke about the offence of the Cross, and he set that over against the Judaizers, who were dogging his steps everywhere and seeking to prejudice his ministry, and at whose hands he was suffering. He 'bore branded on his body the marks of the Lord Jesus' (Galatians vi. 17).

— 48 —

Why? Because of his message of the Cross. He said, 'If I were willing to drop that, I could escape all this suffering; it is the offence of the Cross which is the cause of all the trouble' (Galatians v. 11). And all the way through we see the Jews' unwillingness to admit of a suffering Messiah.

(b) THE WAY OF SELF-EMPTYING

But then it went further than that. It became not only a national issue but a personal one. They would not accept the principle of the Cross in themselves. You find that representative individuals of the nation, who came to the Lord Jesus from time to time, were presented with the offence of the Cross—and off they went again, not prepared to accept it. Nicodemus was very interested in the kingdom which the Messiah was going to set up, which he was expecting and anticipating, but it became a personal matter of the Cross. Before the Lord was through with Nicodemus, He had brought into his full view the serpent lifted up in the wilderness. That was an offence. Another man, who has become known to us as the rich young ruler, went away very sorrowful because of the offence of the Cross. It was no use for the Lord, at that time, before the Cross had actually taken place, to speak in precise terms about it to other than His disciples, but He applied the principle, which is the same thing. He applied the principle to this young man. 'If, as you say, you are interested in the Kingdom and in eternal life, this is the way: the way of emptying—utter self-emptying.' "He went away sorrowful: for he was one that had great possessions" (Matthew xix. 22). The Lord said, "How hardly (with what difficulty) shall they that have riches enter into the kingdom of God!" (Luke xviii. 24). The offence of the Cross finds them out.

Now here, with the Jews as a whole, they were making the kingdom of God an earthly thing on the principles of this world—and do not let us blame them without blaming ourselves. This is our battle right up to date. It is a matter that finds us all out at heart. Oh, you may not be expecting that through your preaching of Christ a temporal kingdom will be set up and you will get a literal crown to wear and a throne to sit upon—that may not be your outlook or mentality; but are we not, almost every day of our lives, in trouble because the Lord hides from us everything that He is doing and starves our souls of their ambition to see things, to have things? Is that not the basis of a great deal of our trouble? We want to see, we want to have, we want the proofs and the evidences. We do really, after all, want a kingdom that can be appraised by our senses of sight and hearing and feeling—a palpable kingdom, the answer in tangible form to all our efforts and labours; and the opposite of that is a tremendous strain upon faith, and sometimes even brings us to a serious crisis.

Why does not the Lord do this and that, which we think He ought to do? It is simply this soul-craving to have proof and demonstration; and this is why, if there is anything built up in Christian work which is obvious, big, impressive, where there is a great thing being organized and a great movement on foot and all is in the realm of something that can be seen, crowds of Christians flock after it; or if there are manifestations, things that seem to be clear proofs, the crowds will be found there. The enemy can carry away multitudes by imitation works of the Holy Ghost in the realm of demonstrations and proofs. We are so impressionable, we must *possess*; and that is exactly the same principle as that which governed the rulers. They were not prepared for the principle of the Cross to be applied in this way—an utter self-emptying, being brought to an end of everything but the Lord Himself.

THE PROPHETS' THEME—KNOWING THE LORD

Now you see that does bring us to the matter of the voices of the prophets. What was the one thing the prophets were always talking about? It was about *knowing the Lord*. The thing that was lacking amongst the Lord's people in the days of the prophets was the knowledge of the Lord. There were plenty of people who were prepared to have the Lord for what He could do for them, but as for the Lord Himself...ah, that was another matter.

What is the Lord after with you and with me? Is He first of all wanting us to do things? The idea of what is of God to-day is chiefly associated with the things which are being done for Him, the work we are engaged in, and so on—that is, with what is objective and outward. But the Lord is not first of all concerned about how much we do. He is far more concerned that, whether we do little or much, every bit of it should come out of a knowledge of Himself. Any amount can be done for the Lord in Christian work and activities, just as you do other work, but it may not proceed from your own deep knowledge of God. The Lord is concerned above all else that we should know Him. "Let not the wise man glory in his wisdom, neither let the mighty man glory in his might, let not the rich man glory in his riches; but let him that glorieth glory in this, that he hath understanding, and knoweth me" (Jeremiah ix. 23, 24, A.R.V.).

May that not explain the very principle of the Cross that is being applied to us? The Lord does not satisfy and gratify; along with lines He seems again and again to be saying, 'No' to quite a lot that we crave for; and, being denied, we often come to the point where we would almost give up everything and allow the biggest questions as to our relationship with the Lord. And yet what He is after all the time, by His denials and withholdings or delays, is to deepen our knowledge of Himself. What matters with the Lord before anything and everything else is not that we should be in any given place doing a lot of Christian work (do not let that stop you serving the Lord!), but that we should be there as one who *knows* the Lord. Our opportunities for serving Him will spring out of our knowledge of Him; He will see to that. The Lord the Spirit is arranging His own work. He knows where need exists, and when He sees someone who can meet that need He can make the contact.

KNOWLEDGE OF THE LORD BASIC
TO ALL USEFULNESS

That is the principle in the New Testament. We see it in the life of the Lord Jesus Himself. That meeting between Christ and the woman of Samaria was not just a casual happening, a pretty story. No, you have principles. The Holy Ghost wrote those narratives, and involved principles in every incident. Here is One who has water to give that the world knows not of, and here is a thirsty woman. God sees to it that the one in need is brought into touch with the One who has the supply. That is a law. If you have not got the supply, it is very largely empty work that is done for the Lord.

The principle of the Cross works out along many lines, in many ways—testing, trying, emptying us, in order to bring us to the place where we know the Lord, and where our joy in the Lord and our enthusiasm and our Christian life are the result of something deeper than the mere momentum produced by doing many things, running about from meeting to meeting, giving addresses, being occupied on the crest of a wave of engagements in Christian work. The Lord does not want it to be like that. I am not saying that you will never be on the crest of a wave, that you will never have your hands full; but the Lord's way of making us useful servants is so to deal with us as to make us know Him, so that, whether occupied in Christian work in an outward way or not, we are there with a knowledge of the Lord. What is so necessary for us is an increasing measure of the preciousness of the Lord to our own hearts; that, whether we are able to do anything or not, He should still remain very precious to us. That is what He wants.

That is very simple, but it is basic to everything. You are there in some place where you cannot be always talking about the Lord, where you can do very little; but if the Lord is precious to you, that is service to Him, and in you He has available a vessel for anything more that He wants. I am sure the Lord will never bring us out and entrust us with responsibilities until He has become very precious to us in the place where we are, even though many other things that we would like are being denied to and withheld from us. It is a principle of the Cross.

Nicodemus comes with all his 'fulness.' He is a man with a great fulness—a ruler of the Jews, in high standing, in a place of influence, and much more. He represents a fulness of a religious kind. Then the Lord virtually says to him: 'You have to let it all go, and start all over again like a newborn babe. You are concerned about the Kingdom of Heaven, but you cannot bring any of that into the Kingdom.' To the rich young ruler He says, in effect, 'You cannot bring your riches in here.' You may have a lot of natural wealth—intellectual, financial, influential, positional, but that does not give you any standing in the Kingdom of Heaven at all. The wealthiest, the fullest, the biggest here in this world receives no more of the glance of the Lord in their direction than the poorest and the weakest. All are brought down here—you must be born again, you must start from zero in this matter of the Kingdom of Heaven. The Kingdom is not a matter of eating and drinking, it is a matter of spiritual measure; and you start spiritual measure by being born of the Spirit. The new life is utterly spiritual from the very first breath—something that was not before, something new.

Spiritual measure is just *knowing the Lord*; that is all. Our standing in the Kingdom of Heaven is simply a matter of knowing the Lord, and if we are going to gain higher place it is not going to be at all by preferences, but by the increase of our spiritual measure. People who count in heaven are spiritual people, and what counts is the degree of their spirituality; and spirituality is knowing the Lord. We may take it that the Lord applies Himself utterly to this matter of bringing us to know *Him*. That is the thing that really does count.

THE CROSS BASIC TO ALL
KNOWLEDGE OF THE LORD

They could not hear the voices of the prophets because the prophets were talking about a suffering Messiah, and there was something inside the people which had closed the door; they were predisposed against anything like that, and so they could not hear. Even the disciples of the Lord Jesus were in that position. When He began to refer to His Cross they said, "Be it far from thee, Lord: this shall never be unto thee" (Matthew xvi. 22). A suffering Messiah? Oh, no! But they did come to the place where the Cross had its very deep application, where it meant an end of everything for them. The Lord precipitated that whole question, and you see them after His crucifixion—they have lost their Messianic Kingdom, they have lost everything, they are stripped and emptied. And then what happened? They began then to *know*, just began to know, and their knowledge grew and grew; but it was of another order entirely. So you find, in the rest of the New Testament, that, in their own history and in their instruction of others, two things go together. They are like the negative and the positive in an electrical circuit—there can be no current without both. The negative is the application of the principle of the Cross, which says No, No, No: an end: death to yourself, death to the world, death to all your own natural life. But the positive is the Holy Ghost, the Spirit of God, mightily present, but always hand in hand with the Cross. With those two acting always together, the negative and the positive—the Cross, and heavenly purpose and heavenly power and effectiveness—you find that there is movement and an ever-growing knowledge of the Lord.

We cannot have the knowledge of the Lord—the most important thing in the mind of God for us—except on the ground of the continuous application of the Cross, and that will go right on to the end. Do not imagine that there will come a day when you have done with the Cross, when the principle of the Cross will no longer be necessary and when you have graduated from the school where the Cross is the instrument of the Lord. Such a day never will be! More and more you will come to recognise the necessity for that Cross. If you are going on into greater fulness of knowledge—I mean spiritual knowledge of the Lord—and therefore greater fulness of usefulness to Him, you must take it as settled that that principle of the Cross is going to be applied more and more deeply as you go on.

Oh, God write that in our hearts! for surely we all know the need of the Cross; and those who have known most about it are conscious most of its need still. We have seen the terrible tragedy of people who knew the message of the Cross in fulness, and who after many years have been a positive contradiction to that very message—marked by self- assertiveness, self-importance, impatience, irritability, so that other people have been unable to live with them. Are you one of those habitually irritable people? I do not mean one of those persons who sometimes is overtaken in a fault. The Lord is patient with the upsets that come here and there along the way, but are we habitually irritable, short-tempered, difficult to live with? That is a denial of the Cross, and that has wrecked the life and work of many a missionary.

The Cross will be applied right on to the end, and, altogether apart from our faults and the things in our constitution and nature which have to be dealt with, in this coming to know the Lord for still greater usefulness we go from death to death on that side of things. We think of some known to us. We marvel at the way the Lord has been able to use them, the large place into which He has put them, what riches He has given them; but of late they have been plunged into depths of death never known before. It is evidently unto something more, something greater still. It is like that; the knowledge of the Lord requires it in an ever-growing way.

KNOWLEDGE AND USEFULNESS
SAFEGUARDED BY THE CROSS

But furthermore, there is no *safe* place, apart from the constant application of the principle of the Cross. Safety absolutely demands it. Nothing is safe in our hands. The more the Lord blesses, the more peril there is. The greatest peril comes when the Lord begins to use us. You may say, 'That does not say very much for our sanctification.'

It certainly does not say very much for 'eradication'! Well, here is Paul. Did that man know anything about the Cross? Would you say he was a crucified man? If he was not, who was? Did he know the Lord? And with all that he knew of the Cross and the Lord, did he know that he needed the Cross to be applied right on to the end? He will definitely place it on record—"...that I should not be exalted overmuch, there was given to me

> **There is no *safe* place, apart from the constant application of the principle of the Cross.**

a thorn in the flesh, a messenger of Satan to buffet me." "That I should not be exalted overmuch"! (II Cor. xii. 7). And mark you, he is saying that because of the great revelation that had been given him. He was caught up into heaven. <u>It is a most perilous thing to be entrusted with Divine riches, so far as our flesh is concerned.</u> The only safe place is where the Cross is still at work, touching all that is ourselves, touching all our independence of action.

Take all these Apostles—take Peter, a man who would act so independently, who liked to do things on his own and do what he wanted to do. We find it cropping up constantly. He is the man who acts without stopping to ask anybody. We have no hint that he ever got into fellowship with his brother disciples and said, 'I am thinking of doing so and so; I would very much like you to pray with me about it, and to tell me what you think; I have no intention of going on unless there is one mind among us.' Peter never did that sort of thing. He got an idea, and off he went. The Lord summed him up very well when He said: "When thou wast young, thou girdedst thyself, and walkedst whither thou wouldest: but when thou shalt be old, thou shalt stretch forth thy hands, and another shall gird thee, and carry thee whither thou wouldest not" (John xxi. 18). That was Peter before the Cross was inwrought in him. But see him afterwards. Why, in those early chapters of Acts, do we read "Peter and John," "Peter and John," "Peter and John"? Well, they are moving together now, there is relatedness. Is it an acknowledgment that Peter felt his need of co-operation and fellowship, that he had seen the perils and disasters into which independent action led him, even when his intentions and motives were of the best? These are just glimpses of how the Cross touches us in our impulsive, independent nature, our self-will, our self-strength. The Cross has to deal with all that to make things safe for God, and to keep us moving in the way of increasing knowledge of the Lord, which, as we have said, lies behind all our value to the Lord, all our usefulness, all our service.

THE CROSS OPENS THE WAY TO FULL KNOWLEDGE OF THE LORD

The Cross is the only way to spiritual knowledge. Important as study of the Word of God may be in its own realm, as laying a foundation for the Holy Spirit to work upon, you never come to a knowledge of the Lord simply by studying the Bible. The Holy Spirit may use what you know of the Bible to teach you much, to explain your experiences, to enable you to understand what the Lord is doing, but you never get this kind of spiritual knowledge merely by study and by teaching.

You must be prepared to let the Cross be so applied to your life that you are broken and emptied and fairly ground to powder—so that you are brought to the place where, if the Lord does not do something, you are finished. If you are prepared for that way, you will get to know the Lord. That is the only way. It cannot be by addresses or lectures. They have their value, but you do not know the Lord spiritually along those lines.

The full knowledge of the Lord is reserved to us who live in this dispensation, because the latter is governed by the Cross. Peter himself had something to say about this:—

"Concerning which salvation the prophets sought and searched diligently, who prophesied of the grace that should come unto you: searching what time or what manner of time the Spirit of Christ which was in them did point unto, when it testified beforehand the sufferings of Christ, and the glories that should follow them. To whom it was revealed, that not unto themselves, but unto you, did they minister these things, which now have been announced unto you...; which things angels desire to look into" (I Peter i. 10-12).

There you have two orders—prophets and angels—who did not know certain things which are revealed to us. The prophets knew much, but they were searching diligently to know something they could not discover. 'What does this mean?' they must have asked themselves. 'The Spirit of God is making us say these things, but what do they mean?' They sought diligently to know that which was reserved for us. Why could they not know? Because full knowledge is based upon the Cross, and the Cross had not taken place then. And angels, too, desire to look into these things. Can it be true? We thought angels knew everything! Surely angels have far more knowledge and intelligence than we have about these things? They do not know. "Which things angels desire to look into." Why do they not know? Angels have had no need of the Cross; the Cross has no meaning for them personally. It is on the basis of the Cross that full knowledge is entered into. Does that need any further argument?

THE CROSS SECURES POSITIVE, NOT ONLY NEGATIVE, RESULTS

So then, the Holy Spirit, in order to bring us to the full knowledge of the Lord and by means of that growing knowledge to make us useful to the Lord, must constantly work by means of the Cross in principle; and my closing word is this. The work is not all negative; the Lord works on a positive basis. You may think that the Lord is always saying No, that He is always against you, that the Cross is suppressive; but no, it is a positive instrument in the hands of the Spirit of God. God is working on a positive line. The fact is that, if ever the Holy Spirit brings us into a new knowing of the meaning of the Cross, He is after something more. That is the law of the Spirit of life.

You must remember that the Lord Jesus, in His resurrection, was not left just where He was before. Before He died He was on this earth, and then He died; and Paul refers to His raising from that death in these words: "the exceeding greatness of his power to us-ward who believe, according to that working of the strength of his might which he wrought in Christ, when he raised him from the dead, and made him to sit at his right hand in the heavenly places, far above all" (Ephesians i. 19-21). The resurrection carries Him through to the "far above all," and the principle of resurrection is always that of rebound—we may go down very deep, more deeply than ever we have known before, but the Spirit of God is intending that that shall issue in our being higher than ever before. So do not be afraid when you are feeling very empty, very finished, very much at the end. Ask the Lord that if this is truly the working of His Cross it shall be successful in what He intends for you; and if it is successful, you will be on higher ground afterward than ever you were before.

THE NEED FOR A DEFINITE TRANSACTION WITH THE LORD

We have said from time to time that the Cross does involve a crisis. For some this may be an overwhelming experience, the biggest thing that has happened in your life, even bigger than your conversion. It was so for some of us as we moved from the apprehension of the substitutionary aspect of the Cross, where we saw only what Christ had done *for* us, to the apprehension of our union with Christ in death, burial and resurrection. Whether or not you have a big crisis which divides your life in two, you must have a point of transaction with the Lord where you recognise that the Cross is in principle an utter, all-inclusive reality that, sooner or later, is going to run to earth the last vestige of that self-life which is the ground of Satan's power. It is best at some point to have this understanding: 'I rejoice in the fact of Thy death for me, and I am saved on the ground of that death and my faith in it. But I died in Thee— that was Thy thought about me as a son of Adam. I could not bear to have all that that means brought to me at once, but I recognise that it has to be worked out as grace enables, and that sooner or later I shall have to come to an utter end; and I therefore commit myself to all Thou dost mean by the Cross.'

A transaction of that kind is necessary. Do not begin to kick when the Lord begins to work it out. He takes you at your word, but He is doing it with the definite object in view of getting you to a higher and fuller knowledge of Himself. Out of that growing knowledge of Him, the growing preciousness of the Lord, all real service will issue. It is not what we *do*, but what we *have*, that is the secret of service.

— 58 —

CHAPTER SIX

THE KINGDOM, AND ENTRANCE INTO IT

"For they that dwell in Jerusalem, and their rulers, because they knew him not, nor the voices of the prophets which are read every sabbath, fulfilled them by condemning him" (Acts xiii. 27).

"Verily I say unto you, Among them that are born of women there hath not arisen a greater than John the Baptist: yet he that is but little in the kingdom of heaven is greater than he. And from the days of John the Baptist until now the kingdom of heaven suffereth violence, and men of violence take it by

force. For all the prophets and the law prophesied until John. And if ye are willing to receive it, this is Elijah, that is to come. He that hath ears to hear, let him hear" (Matthew xi. 11-15).

"The law and the prophets were until John; from that time the gospel of the kingdom of God is preached, and every man entereth violently into it" (Luke xvi. 16).

I THINK WE CAN RECOGNISE that the common link between Acts xiii. 27 and Matthew xi. 13 is "all the prophets." In the one case they heard not the voices of the prophets; in the other it is said (vs. 15), "He that hath ears to hear, let him hear."

THE PROPHETS PROPHESIED
OF THE KINGDOM

First of all, we must understand the meaning of this whole statement in Matthew xi—"all the prophets...prophesied until John." What did they prophesy? Of course, they prophesied many things. One paramount concern in their prophecies was that relating to the coming King and the Kingdom. So much was that so that in the New Testament the matter of the Kingdom is taken for granted. When you open the New Testament and begin to read in the Gospels, you find that no explanation is given. The Kingdom is not introduced as something of which people were unaware. You find from amongst the people those who came to the Lord Jesus and used the very phrase, and you find the Lord Himself, although the matter was not mentioned by others who came to Him, using the phrase 'the Kingdom' without any introduction or explanation.

Nicodemus was a case in point. We have nothing in the narrative to indicate that Nicodemus said anything at all about the Kingdom. He started by saying: "Rabbi, we know that thou art a teacher come from God." There was nothing about the Kingdom in that. The Lord Jesus interrupted there and said: "Except one be born anew, he cannot see the kingdom of God" (John iii. 2, 3). Evidently that was the thing that was in the mind of Nicodemus, and the Lord knew it. You see, it is a thing taken for granted in the New Testament; and although later (as we find in the book of the Acts and subsequently) the true heavenly explanation is given, or there is some teaching concerning its true meaning, the Kingdom is something that is already very much in the minds of the Jewish people, and of course it has come from the prophets. The prophets had much to say concerning the Kingdom, and some of them had something very definite to say about the King. We will not try to prove that. It is a statement which you can easily verify.

What did the prophets prophesy? Inclusively, they prophesied concerning the King and the Kingdom. What was the culmination of the prophets in that comprehensive connection? It was John the Baptist. He gathered them all up; he was, so to speak, the inclusive prophet. What was John the Baptist? He was the terminal or turning point between all that had been and that which was now going to be, between the Old Testament and the New. That is the statement here—"all...prophesied until John." Until John; now—from John. What was the message of John? "Repent ye; for the kingdom of heaven is at hand" (Matthew iii. 2). But alongside that, the great outstanding note of John is, "Behold, the Lamb of God, that taketh away the sin of the world!" (John i. 29). Those are not two different things; they are one. "The kingdom...is at hand": "Behold, the Lamb of God!"

THE KINGDOM PRESENT IN CHRIST

What was the issue, then, from John's time—the issue which sprang into new meaning, new force, because it had become an immediate one; no longer that of prophecy but now the issue of actuality? It was the Kingdom of Heaven. "The law and the prophets were until John: from that time the gospel of the kingdom of God is preached." The prophets had prophesied it; now it is preached as having come, and having come with "the Lamb of God, that taketh away the sin of the world."

What, then, is the Kingdom of Heaven? We have led up to this step by step, and when we answer this final question we shall see clearly what it was that these Jewish rulers and dwellers in Jerusalem never saw, though they heard the prophets week by week.

I am going to press the challenge of this again. I feel that it is a very solemn thing that ever the Kingdom of Heaven should have come near to anyone. You see, the Lord is eventually going to judge everyone on their opportunity. The opportunity has been given—and contact is opportunity. The very availability of the Kingdom is opportunity. What is done with opportunity? The Lord Jesus walked in the midst of the Jewish nation three and a half years. His very presence among them was their opportunity—and what a terrible, terrible consequence followed their failure to make good their opportunity!

Now there may be someone in this category who reads these words. Through reading them, there has become available to you, even if never before (but surely we could hardly say that), the gospel of Jesus Christ—the knowledge of the fact of the Lord Jesus and His Cross. To have ever had that within your reach is enough to settle your eternal destiny. If the Kingdom of Heaven is come near—within the compass and range of your life, to your knowledge—that is the ground upon which your eternal destiny may be settled. Of course, there was very much more in the case of these people, and their condemnation was so much the more. The prophets prophesied in their hearing, and yet because of something in their own make-up, because of some reaction from themselves, the rulers and the people never heard what they were hearing; they never recognised that here was something which had very great implications, and that they must find out what those implications really were. They did not take the attitude—'If there is something here which concerns me, I must know what it is.'

You could hardly ask for less than that, could you?—but the very absence of that kind of reaction to the presence of the gospel, as I have said, may be the ground upon which judgment will take place. It did in their case, and a terrible judgment it was! What a judgment, these two thousand years of Jewish history! "Your house is left unto you desolate" (Matthew xxiii. 38). Was there ever a story of more awful desolation than the story of the Jews since then? But, even so, that is only a *parable* of desolation; something here on this earth. What must desolation in the spiritual and eternal sense mean—forsaken of God, and knowing it? It is a solemn message, and of course it paves the way to this other part, the "violent" entering into the Kingdom. This is something to take seriously, something about which you cannot afford to be careless or indifferent.

What is the Kingdom? The answer to that can be given in three or four quite brief statements. What did the Kingdom of Heaven prove to be? I repudiate that system of interpretation which claims that a literal, earthly, temporal kingdom was offered to the Jews at this time. I do not believe it. It would have been a poor sort of thing for the people of whom we read in the Gospels to have had the kingdom in their hands—not much glory or satisfaction to God in them! No, I repudiate the interpretation of a temporal kingdom being offered to Israel by Jesus at that time. But what did the Kingdom of Heaven, which was preached in the days of John the Baptist, prove to be and to mean, as the Lord Jesus interpreted it, and later the Apostles?

WHAT THE KINGDOM IS
(a) A NEW LIFE

First of all, the Kingdom of Heaven was a new life, altogether other than that which men knew anything about in all their history from Adam onward. That is what the Lord meant in His own first reference to the Kingdom, when speaking to Nicodemus about his soul's need. "Except one be born anew, he cannot see the kingdom of God"—because it is another life that has come in, as by a birth. It is not just the energizing of an old life. It is not just the swinging over of an old life into new interests, turning from one line of interest to another, from one system of occupation to another: once you were all out for the world, and now with the same life and interest you are all out for Christianity. No, it is another, different life, a life that never was, given from God Himself. The very essence of the Kingdom of Heaven is that it is a heavenly nature in a heavenly life, given as a distinct gift at a crisis. Another life—that is the Kingdom, to begin with.

(b) A NEW RELATIONSHIP

It is a new relationship, a relationship with God: which is not simply that now we become interested in God—that God becomes an object in our consideration and we swing over from one relationship to another because now we have taken up Christianity. No, it is a relationship which is of the essence of this very life itself. We have an altogether new and different consciousness, so far as our relationship to God is concerned.

The great truth of the Gospels, especially as emphasized in the Gospel by John, is that a new revelation of relationship with God has come by Jesus Christ. "I manifested thy name unto the men whom thou gavest me out of the world" (John xvii. 6). That name, of which He is always speaking, represented a new relationship—"Father"; not in the sense of a general and universal fatherhood of God and brotherhood of man, but a specific, new relationship which comes about only by entering of the Holy Spirit into the life in a definite, critical act. "God sent forth the Spirit of His Son into our hearts, crying, Abba, Father" (Galatians iv. 6). When did that happen with you? What was the very first lisp of your new life? "Father!"—uttered out of a new consciousness. Not now a God who is afar off, unthinkable, all-terrible, of whom you are afraid; no, "Father!" When we are "born of the Spirit," there is brought about an entirely new relationship.

(c) A NEW CONSTITUTION

Then the Kingdom of Heaven is a new constitution. I am not think-ing now of a new set of laws and regulations, but of a new constitution as far as you and I are concerned. We are constituted anew, with an entirely new set of capacities which make possible things which were never possible before. It ought to be recognised—and I would have you lay this to heart anew—that the child of God, the member of the Kingdom of Heaven, is the embodiment of a miracle, which means that there are super-natural possibilities and capacities in every such one. What tremen-dous things go on in the history of a child of God! When we see fully and clearly at last, we shall recognise them to have been nothing less than Divine miracles again and again. We do not know all the forces which are bent upon the destruction of a child of God, and how much his preserving through to the end represents an exercise of the almighty power of God. Some of us know a little about that: that our very survival is because God has exercised His power over other immense hostile powers, that we are kept by the power of God—and that it takes the power of God to keep us!

The inception of the life of the child of God is a miracle. 'How can a man be born again?' There is no answer to that question except that God does it. "How can this man give us his flesh to eat?" (John vi. 52). That is, how can the child of God be supported throughout, without anything here to help, to succour, to nourish? There is no answer to that either, except that God does it; and if He does not, the child of God, because of the extra forces centred upon him or her for destruction, will simply go under. The consummation of the life of the child of God will be equally a miracle. "How are the dead raised? and with what manner of body do they come?" (1 Corinthians xv. 35). The answer to that is the same—God alone is going to do it.

The whole matter is a miracle from start to finish. It is a new constitution, having in it possibilities and capacities which are altogether above and beyond the highest level of human abilities; that is, above and over the whole kingdom of earth and nature.

(d) A NEW VOCATION

Further, it is a new vocation. It is something for which to live, something in which to serve, something to bring into operation. It becomes the sphere and the means of a new life-ministry and -purpose. The very consciousness of a truly born-again child of God is like this—'Now I know why I am alive! I have been wondering all along why I was born; I have grumbled about it, and felt I was hardly done by in being brought into this world without being consulted as to whether I wanted to come; but now I see there is purpose in it—I have something to live for!' A truly born-again child of God goes off and tells people that, after all, it is worth being alive! He has discovered, behind everything else, that which has Divine intent and meaning—it never existed as an active thing until he was born anew and entered into the Kingdom. The Kingdom of Heaven is a new vocation, a new sense of life-purpose. It gives to life a meaning. That is the Kingdom.

Is that not altogether a different idea from that which would make the Kingdom a place with certain laws and regulations—'You must' and

'You must not'—something objective? "The kingdom of God is within you" (Luke xvii. 21), and it is after this kind.

(e) A NEW GRAVITATION—TO HEAVEN, NOT EARTH

It is moreover something from above, and that surely implies that it is transcendent in every way. It is something that lives, and it brings life up on to a higher level. That is, if the new life comes from above, from heaven, it will always gravitate back to its source, and if this new life works in us, it will be lifting us, pulling us upward to God. It will so work that we shall feel first of all that this world is not our home. It was our home; everything for us was here until that happened; we saw nothing beyond. Now we do not belong to it, we belong somewhere else; and in some strange way we are steadily moving further and further away from this earth. We find that we become less comfortable here every day. You are in the Kingdom if you have something like that experience. If you can be comfortable and happy and content to go on here you ought to have grave doubts as to where you are as regards the Kingdom. But if you are increasingly conscious that inwardly the distance is growing between you and all that is here, then the Kingdom is truly at work, the Kingdom of Heaven has come.

THE KINGDOM COME BUT ALSO COMING

Now, another thing: the Kingdom has come, but it is always coming. We have entered, but we ought to be always entering. There is a little word at the end of the letter to the Hebrews—"Wherefore, receiving a kingdom that cannot be shaken..." (Hebrews xii. 28). The literal sense there is "being in the course or process of receiving a kingdom that cannot be shaken..." It has come, but it is coming; and it is at that point that I think we all need to recognise a difference, to discriminate between two things—between conversion and salvation.

Have you ever made that distinction? There is all the difference between conversion and salvation. Conversion is a crisis, something that happens perhaps suddenly, in a moment, and it is done. Salvation? That is something that has commenced; but you find also that the New Testament speaks about "receiving the end of your faith, even the salvation of your souls" (I Peter i. 9), thus indicating that salvation is still future. Some people have built a false doctrine upon this, teaching that you cannot know you are saved until you are at the end, because it is spoken of in the future tense. But we are saved, and we are being saved. We have entered the Kingdom by conversion, but salvation is a far greater thing than conversion. Oh, salvation is a vast thing, and is only another word for the Kingdom—the Kingdom coming all the time. A spiritual babe who has just received Divine life has not got everything, except potentially. It has conversion, it has new birth. Would you say that a little babe has everything it is intended to have? Potentially, in the life, all is there. But how much more there is to be known of what that life implies, of all that it carries with it and may lead to, of all the capacities that are there!

That is the difference between conversion and salvation. The Kingdom is a vast kingdom—"His kingdom is an everlasting kingdom" (Daniel iv. 3). "Of the increase of his government...there shall be no end" (Isaiah ix. 7). 'No end' simply means eternally expansive. Can you make just a geographical matter of that? Surely not. It must be spiritual—the vast inexhaustible resources of God for His own people. It will take eternity to know and to explore all those resources, the dimensions of His Kingdom.

THE KINGDOM SUFFERS VIOLENCE

Now, having in a imperfect way considered what the prophets were talking about and what you and I have come into touch with, let us see what can be missed. Let us look at these other words: "The law and the prophets were until John: from that time the gospel of the kingdom of God is preached, and every man entereth violently into it" (Luke xvi. 16). "From the days of John the Baptist until now the kingdom of heaven suffereth violence, and men of violence take it by force" (Matthew xi. 12). It "suffereth violence." That does not simply mean that it permits of violence. It really means that it calls for violence, and it is men of violence that take it by force. Luke puts it "entereth violently."

Here is the spirit of citizenship in that Kingdom—"by force." Why? This is not merely an appeal to be in earnest—though it certainly includes that, seeing what a tremendous thing this Kingdom is, and what an immense loss will be suffered if we do not take it seriously. But you see, the Lord Jesus is speaking as in the midst of things which are constantly opposing. There is a whole organized system, expressing tremendous prejudice. He said to them on one occasion: "Woe unto you, scribes and Pharisees, hypocrites! because ye shut the kingdom of heaven against men: for ye enter not in yourselves, neither suffer ye them that are entering in to enter" (Matthew xxiii. 13). There is everything, from devil and men, to obstruct; to enter in requires violence. If you can be hindered, you will be hindered. If you are going to be easy going, you will give to antagonistic forces all the ground that they want to put you out.

That is why I pointed out that it is not only a once-for-all entering into the Kingdom, but it is a continuous entering. The Kingdom is so much bigger than conversion. Of course, if you are going to be saved at all—I mean saved initially—you will have to mean business for that. You will have to make it a desperate matter, because there will be everything to stop you. But the Kingdom means a very great deal more than merely getting into it, far more than being converted. There is a great deal more in the purpose of God for our lives than we have ever imagined, and if we are to enter into that, violence has to characterize us. We must desperately mean business, and come to the place where we say: 'Lord, I am set upon all that Thou dost mean in Christ. I am set upon that, and I am not going to allow other people's prejudices or suspicions or criticisms to get in the way; I am not going to allow any man-made system to hinder me; I am going right on with Thee for all Thy purpose. I am going to do violence to everything that would get in the way.' It calls for violence, and we have to do a lot of violence to get all that God wills for us.

> **I am going to do violence to everything that would get in the way.**

Oh how easily many lives are side-tracked, simply because they are not desperate enough! They are caught in things which limit—things which may be good, that may have something of God in them, but which none the less are limiting things, and do not represent a wide open way to all God's purpose. The only way for us to come into all that the Lord means—not only into what we have seen but into all that He has purposed—is to be desperate, to be men of violence; to be men who say, 'By God's grace, nothing and no one, however good, is going to stand in my way; I am going on with God.' Have that position with the Lord, and you will find that God meets you on that ground.

No men—not even Paul himself—knew all that they were going to know. Paul was constantly getting fuller unveilings of that unto which he was called. He received something fairly strong and rich at the beginning; then, later, he was shown unspeakable things (II Corinthians xii. 4). He was growing in apprehension. But why? Because he was a man of violence. God meets us like that. "With the perverse thou wilt shew thyself froward" (Psalms xviii. 26). That, in principle, means that God will be to you what you are to Him. He will mean business if you mean business. There is a vast amount in the Kingdom that we have never suspected. Do believe that. There is more for all of us to know than anybody on this earth knows—far more than the very greatest saints, the most advanced Christians, know of the purpose of God.

Paul intimates that. In his Philippian letter he makes it clear that, even at the end of his life, he has yet to apprehend, he needs still to know. "That I may know..." (Philippians iii. 10). There is far more to know. Do you believe that? Are you going to allow your life simply to be boxed up within the measure that you know, or within the measure of other people? No—it is the measure of Christ that is God's end. "Till we all attain unto the unity of the faith, and of the knowledge of the Son of God, unto a fullgrown man, unto the measure of the stature of the fulness of Christ" (Ephesians iv. 13). No movement, no society, no evangelical organization, no church on this earth has come to that yet, but that is the objective in view. But God requires, in order to bring us to fulness, that we be men of violence, that we really mean business, that we say to everything that gets in the way—and oh, the plausible voices, which nevertheless are subtly influenced by prejudices!—'Stand thou aside; I am going on with God, I am going to allow nothing to stand in the way.'

"The gospel of the kingdom is preached." Can you imagine those Judaizers speaking to the people about Jesus? 'Be careful; mind you don't get caught! Our advice to you is to steer clear of that—don't get into too close touch with Him!' All that was going on. Paul was up against it all the time. He was tracked down throughout his journeys by these very people who, following on his heels, said, 'Be careful—it is dangerous!' The Lord Himself experienced the same kind of thing; and He said: "the kingdom... suffereth violence." It calls for violence; you will not get in to begin with, and you will certainly not get in in growing fulness, unless you are one of those people who do violence to everything that stands in the way of God's full purpose as revealed in Christ. You will not even know what that purpose is, God will not be able to reveal to you the next part of it, unless He finds that you are one after this kind—entering in violently.

Are you like that? Well, if we are passive, there is everything to be lost; if we mean business, there is everything to be gained. The Lord make us men and women like that, lest we be numbered among those of whom it is said that they "have ears to hear, and hear not" (Ezekiel xii. 2).

SEVEN

THE CONTRAST BETWEEN THE OLD DISPENSATION AND THE NEW

"For they that dwell in Jerusalem, and their rulers, because they knew Him not, nor the voices of the prophets which are read every sabbath, fulfilled them by condemning him" (Acts xiii. 27).

IN A WAY, THAT VERSE IS THE KEY to the whole of the book of Acts, for this book is really an interpretation and exhibition of the principle that is at the heart of that statement—that is, that there is the Bible with its verbal statements, its record of utterances and activities of God through men, and it can be read and re-read for a lifetime, as it was in the case of the people referred to here, and yet the real significance may be missed. In other words, there is in it something more than the actual verbal statements. You may have the statements, the letter, the volume, the whole record, and you may know it as such, as these Jewish rulers did, and yet you may be missing the way, you may be moving on a plane altogether other than that which God intended. This book of the Acts, from beginning to end, shows that there was something more in the mind of God when He inspired men of old to speak and to write than is discernible in the actual words which they used, and which requires the activity of the Spirit of God if it is to be heard and grasped and understood, and if it is going to work out as things worked out in this book— in power, in effectiveness.

There is much of the Old Testament in the book of the Acts, and in the New Testament as a whole. The prophets are very much quoted, but see the difference between the effect of the words as used in the book of the Acts and the effect upon those who merely heard or read the actual utterances of the prophets. The Holy Ghost has come; and He is not making another Bible, He is using the old one; but it is a new book with a new meaning and a new effect, and you are amazed at times at the way in which He uses Scripture. You never saw that it meant that; it is something altogether beyond a former apprehension, although you knew that Scripture quite well in a way. There is a difference, and it is a crucial one.

So these people in Jerusalem and their rulers heard every Sabbath the prophets, but failed to hear their voice. They missed something—the voice of God coming through, the meaning of God in what was being said, as distinct from the mere statements. It is possible for a company to be gathered together and for one to be speaking the word of the Lord, and for some merely to hear the words and go away and say, 'He said so and so,' repeating what was actually said in verbal statements. It is at the same time possible for others to say, 'I never saw it like that before; I knew that passage of Scripture, but I never saw that!' Something, not only of a fresh recognition but of living value, has been detected. That is the difference between the words of the prophets and the voice of God through the words of the prophets.

So, as I have said, this verse in chapter xiii is, in a way, a key to this whole book. It makes this discrimination, which is so very important, between the letter and the spirit, between the statements and the Divine meaning in the statements. One is death and gets nowhere. The other is life and goes right through.

ALL PROPHECY POINTS
TO THE LORD JESUS

Let us now glance at the book of Acts. We go right back to the first chapter with this principle in mind. It might be well for us to be reminded, in parenthesis, that, speaking broadly, the whole Bible (but for a few verses) closes upon a comprehensive statement about this very matter. In Revelation xix 10, we are told that "the testimony of Jesus is the spirit of prophecy." What does that mean? It simply means this—that all the way through the Bible, from the beginning onward, there has been a predictive element in this sense, an element of implication, something implied beyond the actual words said at the time. In it all there has been a pointer onward. It may be an historic incident, something quite local and immediate in itself as to time, place and persons concerned, but in no part of the Bible is only the local and present in view. There is something more—there is an implication, there is a pointer onward; and if you could see where all these pointers point to, you would find it was Jesus. He is implied in everything, everywhere.

When we speak of prophecy, do not let us limit our thoughts to certain times and certain men of the Old Testament. True, we have been, and are very often, occupied with the prophets whose books are included in the 'prophetic' section of the Old Testament, but we have to expand beyond that. Moses was called a prophet (Deuteronomy xviii. 15), and Samuel was a prophet (I Samuel iii. 20), and even David in the New Testament is called a prophet (Acts ii. 30). The spirit of prophecy embraces more than a certain class of men whom we designate prophets. The spirit of prophecy goes right back, as far back as Enoch; no, further back than that—to Genesis iii. 15, concerning the seed of the woman: that is the spirit of prophecy. So if we remember that prophecy is something so far-reaching and all-inclusive, and bearing upon the Lord Jesus, I hope we are able to see something of Divine meaning as being more than verbal statement.

With that parenthesis, let us come to the first chapter of the Acts.

THE HOLY SPIRIT'S HIDDEN MEANING
IN THE SCRIPTURES

"They therefore, when they were come together, asked him saying, Lord, dost thou at this time restore the kingdom to Israel?" (Acts i. 6).

We pointed out in a previous chapter how much the prophets were occupied with this matter of the Kingdom. These disciples of the Lord Jesus had their whole idea of the Kingdom from the prophets, and so their question is based upon a certain kind of mental apprehension of the teaching of the prophets. They had deduced certain things from what the prophets said, and they bring this question even at this late hour—"Dost thou at this time restore the kingdom to Israel? And he said unto them, It is not for you to know times and seasons, which the Father hath set within his own authority. But ye shall receive power, when the Holy Spirit is come upon you; and ye shall be my witnesses both in Jerusalem, and in all Judaea and Samaria, and unto the uttermost part of the earth. And when He had said these things, as they were looking,"—He restored the Kingdom, ascended His throne? No—"he was taken up; and a cloud received him out of their sight" (Acts i. 6-9).

Everything begins there in the way of spiritual understanding, because this statement of the Lord Jesus indicated that a new dispensation was being inaugurated which was different from that which the disciples had expected from the teaching of the prophets. This was the dispensation of the Holy Spirit, and they were going to discover that the Holy Spirit had meanings about the Old Testament prophecies which they had never imagined were there. Not until the Holy Spirit took hold of the Word of God did they know the prophets at all. And then we shall see that when He really took hold of the Scriptures and began to apply them and open them up and give the Divine meaning, things happened which not only were unexpected but were utterly contrary and opposed to the fixed mentality of the disciples, and which required a complete shattering of their mentality, the abandonment of established positions on their part. It is tremendously challenging if the Holy Spirit gets hold of the Word of God and then gets hold of us. There are going to be revolutionary changes in our whole outlook and procedure, and this book of the Acts is just full of that.

THE COMING OF THE SPIRIT—A
NEW ORDER INTRODUCED

It is the dispensation, or stewardship, of the Holy Ghost. The words 'dispensation' and 'stewardship' mean an economy, an order; how things are done in this régime. We find that, in this dispensation, when the Holy Spirit came, He began to change things, because He was in charge. You may become a member of the staff of a business, and when you arrive you find things are done in such and such a way. Times are set and fixed like this; this is how things are done in this régime. And then a new Managing Director arrives, and he sees this prevailing order, and he registers at once that it is an imperfect system, that is not producing the fullest results for which the business exists. He begins quietly but very strongly to take charge, and things begin to change, and the old set people who have been in that regime for years do not like these changes, and they begin to kick. They will not have it; they revolt and begin to fight against this new order. Some, who are more open-spirited, who are not so fixed and settled, begin to see his mind, his vision, and although they stumble on difficulties from time to time, and come up against the implications of this tremendous change—like Peter, over the visit to Cornelius (Acts x)—and it wants just a little battle to get over the old prejudice, nevertheless, they have their battle, get over their difficulties, and fall into line, and so the great change takes place with wonderful results. Things begin to happen; the original purpose of the business is now beginning, in a wonderful way, to be realised and fulfilled.

That is exactly what happened when the Holy Spirit came in on the day of Pentecost. There was an existing, fixed, established order, but it was not reaching God's end. It was not, as we say, 'delivering the goods.' The Holy Ghost came, with all the full knowledge of the Divine mind; He entered in and began His work of realising the real Divine concept; He took hold. So He divided the people. Some—these that dwelt in Jerusalem, and their rulers—would not have the new order. Well, all right—they lose it all. But others came into the fellowship of the Holy Ghost, "joined unto the Lord...one spirit" (I Corinthians vi. 17), with wonderful results.

A VITAL CONTRAST—THE LETTER
AND THE SPIRIT OF SCRIPTURE

The point is: first of all, it is a new dispensation; and next, the Holy Ghost is in charge. His being in charge has to be recognised, with all that it means. And, being in charge, by His activities He reveals and evolves the very object of God from all eternity, and seeks to bring it out in this dispensation. As for the cleavage—well, it was an historic cleavage then, but it is a cleavage which spiritually has been going on all through the dispensation. It is a dividing between men of the letter and men of the spirit. That movement, that tendency, toward a fixed position is constantly recurring, bringing that which is of God into imprisonment, within organized limitations which frustrate the whole counsel of God. I have an article before me—I wish I could quote it all; I cannot—but there are some things in it which express what is in my heart better than anything that I could say myself. It was written by a Member of the British Parliament.

'There are many classifications into which men and women may be divided—as upper, middle or lower class; rich, well-to-do and poor; religious, sceptical and atheist;...and so forth and so on. But, as I think, the only categorization which really matters is that which divides men as between the Servants of the Spirit and the Prisoners of the Organization. That classification, which cuts right across all other classifications, is indeed the fundamental one. The idea, the inspiration, originates in the internal world, the world of the Spirit...the idea having embodied itself in the organization, the organization then proceeds gradually to slay the idea which gave it birth. In the field of religion a prophet, an inspired man, will see a vision of truth. He expresses that vision as best he may in words. Upon what his disciples understand of the prophet's message, an organization, a church will be built. The half-understood message will crystalize into a creed. Before long the principle concern of the church will be to sustain itself as an organization. To this end any departure from the creed must be controverted and, if necessary, suppressed as heresy. In a few score or a few hundred years what was conceived as a vehicle of a new and higher truth has become a prison for the souls of men. And men are murdering each other for the love of God.

'One moral to be drawn, it would not be wholly facetious to suggest, might be that the first rule for any organization should be a rule providing for its dissolution within a limited period of time...When we are members of an organization, as such, our attitude to it should be one of partial detachment. We must be above it even while we are in it. We should reckon on being in almost perpetual rebellion within it. Above all we should regard all loyalties to organization as tentative and provisional. We must be Servants of the Spirit, not Prisoners of the Organization. We must keep in touch with the sources of life, not lose ourselves in the temporary vehicles.

'This world is a bridge. Ye shall pass over it, but ye shall build no houses upon it.'

Is that not just what you have in the Acts and all the way through—the crystallizing of our apprehension of truth, our interpretation, the partial perception, the statement in the letter, something fixed, embodying that which was of the Spirit of God in the beginning, but not allowing it to go beyond those bounds now? Anything more, anything other than that, is called heresy; this is the last word. It may be embodied in an organization, in what is called a church, a sect, a denomination, and if you go beyond that, well, you are said to be all wrong. The great difference between men of the organization and men of the Spirit is what you have here in the Book of the Acts.

THE LORDSHIP OF THE SPIRIT
ESSENTIAL TO PROGRESS

The point is this: the fulness of Divine purpose demands that the Holy Spirit be continually in charge, that He be allowed to be completely in the place of government, and that we do not put anything in His place—nothing whatsoever; not a 'church,' not a fixed order—so that at any point or in any way we could say, 'That is not what we teach, that is not what we have been brought up to believe, that is not what our church believes and teaches? To do that is to put something in the way of the Holy Ghost. The Holy Ghost must be in charge and must be free. It was on those very points that the Apostles themselves had firstly their battles and then their enlargements. We shall see that as we go on. The full Divine purpose is going to take shape when the Holy Spirit is in charge with us.

And then there is something infinitely greater than times and seasons. Be careful about times and seasons; they have a wonderful and pernicious way of bringing you into limitations. Many people are dwelling in times and seasons. But they have done that all the way through the centuries. Let us watch, observe, take note; but be careful. Things have been happening, for example, in Palestine. We were told that the times of the Gentiles ended when General Allenby entered Jerusalem; that a new Caesar had arrived to reconstitute the Roman Empire when Mussolini set up his great empire in Rome! That sort of thing has been going on for centuries, and it is all based upon times and seasons.

The point is this—not that there are no times and seasons, not that there are not movements in the plan of God which have their particular characteristics and can be noted, but that there is something infinitely greater than that. It is the heavenly and not the earthly aspect that is in view in the Book of the Acts. That is why I stayed at that point, "When he had said these things...he was taken up." From that point it became a heavenly matter. Later the apostle Paul will use a phrase like this: "The Spirit searcheth all things, yea, the deep things of God" (I Corinthians ii. 10). "The Spirit searcheth...the deep things of God": that is something transcendently greater than times and seasons; and if the Holy Spirit really is in charge, there is no fathoming what God has to reveal. "Things which eye saw not, and ear heard not, and which entered not into the heart of man." It is out there, into that vast realm, that the Holy Spirit would bring us, and we must be very careful that we do not clamp down on the Holy Spirit with man-made, man-constituted institutions. We must keep out in the open with the Spirit, and it is there that our surprises will begin—yes, and our very real discipline.

THE PROPHETS' ULTIMATE MEANING
SPIRITUAL AND HEAVENLY

Those referred to in Acts xiii. 27, or those of whom they were typical, had a kind of apprehension of the Scriptures. There was no doubt at all about their devotion to the Word of God. They were fundamentalists of a rabid kind, as far as the inspiration of the Scriptures was concerned.

They stickled for the Scriptures; they dotted all the i's and crossed all the t's. Many among them were particular about the smallest detail in the realm of outward observances, even to the point of fussy fastidiousness. Because the law ordained that a tithe of all the fruit of the land was the Lord's, they tithed meticulously even their mint and other herbs—but at the same time overlooked the things that were inward and which mattered much more to the Lord, such as judgment, mercy and faith (Matthew xxiii. 23). That was their apprehension, their mentality, their position. They saw everything on the horizontal. It was a matter of the exact technique of Scripture.

What was the result? Well, they were perpetuating an earthly system with the Word of God. Their 'church' was the 'church of Israel,' the 'Israelitish church'—and you can put in the place of Israel any other denominational title that you like. That church had its own particular forms, its vestments, its ritual, its liturgy, and all according to the Scriptures. It had its reading of the prophets every Sabbath. It had the whole system; but it was right down here on this earth and as dead as anything could be. It was purely formal; it was not getting through to God's end at all. Scriptural, in a sense, though it was, it was failing to realise the eternal counsels of God. When the Holy Ghost came, He did not sweep away the prophets, the Old Testament. He took them up and showed that there was something more—something more than all that earthly, perfect technique of the Word of God, with all its accompaniments—without which all that other would have to be set aside. And it is going to be set aside. It fails to reach God's end, therefore it passes out; and that is the issue of the Book of Acts—the great transition. There is a Divine meaning back of all that, and when you have the Divine meaning, you can dispense with the other—it can go. If you have the thing in the really spiritual sense and realm, in the living and heavenly way, it does not matter about the other; that just drops out and falls away.

That is what happened in the Book of the Acts. You can hardly see the point at which it happened, but there is such a point. The Apostles did go on attending the temple and the synagogues for a little while, and then they ceased to do so. They were continuing for a time, but then it was as though they were steadily, quietly, moving out, and eventually they were out. Something had happened. They had come into the real thing and the initial thing had gone. The one led to the other, but it had served its purpose. They came into the heavenly good and meaning of it all; it was not a matter of technique now.

There are many who will say about the fixed orders and rituals: 'Of course, we do not regard this as everything; it is only symbolic. We do remember that it implies and points to something else, and it is that something else we are thinking of.' Yes, but is it not true that, when the Holy Ghost comes, as He came then, and gets possession, and you go on with Him, more and more the emphasis of the merely outward and earthly and temporal aspects of Christianity fade away, and you become increasingly occupied with the glory of the reality? The Jesus of history gives full place to the Jesus of the Spirit, of heaven. That is exactly what is meant by "the voices of the prophets."

> **Even New Testament Christianity can be reduced again to an earthly system of exact technique.**

So, on the day of Pentecost, you start with Joel. Everybody in Jerusalem was saying, "What meaneth this?" (Acts ii. 12). They were all bewildered, without any understanding or perception; and Peter, with the eleven, stood up and said: "This is that which hath been spoken through the prophet Joel" (vs. 16). "This is that..." What a crushing blow it was to tradition, what an upheaval it created in Israel, this with its implications of Jesus of Nazareth! And the Apostle went on, quoting freely from the Old Testament. He quoted David. That sermon of his on the day of Pentecost was just full of Old Testament quotations. But who ever saw that—who ever knew that that was the meaning of it!

You see the point. It is something that really needs to come to us with tremendous force, because even New Testament Christianity can be reduced again to an earthly system of exact technique. You can write your manuals on New Testament procedure. You can have it exactly according to the letter but it is all on the horizontal, it becomes legalistic, it ties up the Holy Ghost. Although the intention may have been to be more exactly according to Scripture, that the Lord might have a fuller way, it does not always result in that. The whole thing must be baptized in the Holy Ghost and lifted clean off the earthly level, becoming something entirely heavenly.

OUR RESPONSIBILITY TO YIELD TO THE SPIRIT

Now I think we can rightly say that, when the disciples asked, "Lord, dost thou at this time restore the kingdom to Israel?" they were seriously and genuinely exercised. The Scriptures must be fulfilled; what was written must happen. I think the disciples were very much occupied with this, burdened and perplexed; they wanted to know how things were going to work out. The Lord said, in effect: 'Do not worry about that. The Holy Ghost is coming and He will take all responsibility for everything–times and seasons and everything else. He is coming with the whole purpose of God in His hands, and He will work it out. You can be at rest–it is all right.' Those who get this earthly idea and conception of a system become terribly worried and burdened to work it out–burdened with the awful responsibility of this 'New Testament Church,' of having things exactly as the Scriptures say! If the Holy Ghost were in charge, the burden would go. *He* is doing it. All that we are called upon to do is to get into the hands of the Holy Spirit, get completely free from all this harness, free to the Spirit of God. Matters will work out all right.

And even if the Holy Spirit comes up against some stones in us and for a time there is some conflict, He is more than equal to that situation. He is more than equal to Peter and his never having eaten anything unclean. When the Lord gave Peter that vision of the sheet let down with all manner of fourfooted beasts and creeping things and said, "Rise, Peter; kill and eat," Peter in effect quoted Scripture to the Lord; he quoted Leviticus xi, with its commandments concerning the unclean beasts which must not be eaten. 'Lord here is Scripture for my position; my position is soundly founded upon the Word of God!' What are you going to do with that? Now listen–*I am not saying nor even implying that the*

Holy Ghost will ever call upon us to do something contrary to the Scriptures. He never will. But He will very often show us that the Scriptures mean something that we never saw them to mean. Leviticus xi had a meaning that Peter had not seen. He had taken the letter and the literal meaning of those things. He never saw the Divine, spiritual meaning at the back of that. Cornelius had never received the Holy Spirit, and therefore an angel spoke to him. Peter had received the Holy Spirit on the day of Pentecost, and it was the Spirit who was speaking to Peter. The Holy Ghost had this matter in hand, and was dealing with the difficulties in Peter, even in his fundamentalism, to lift him off a merely temporal, earthly ground to a heavenly. Peter was living under an open heaven; and there are tremendous changes when you get there. It does not all happen at once.

THE HOLY SPIRIT 'UPON' AND 'IN'

Just one further word for the present. You notice here that there was a double operation of the Holy Spirit. In chapter ii, the Spirit lighted 'upon' them. These cloven tongues as of fire sat upon them; and then it says, "They were all filled with the Holy Spirit, and began to speak with other tongues, as the Spirit gave them utterance." 'Upon' and 'in.' I do not want to be technical, contradicting what we have been saying about too much technique, but there is a meaning in the 'upon' and the 'in.' The coming 'upon' is the sovereignty of the Holy Spirit in relation to God's eternal purpose. That is, the Holy Spirit has come as the custodian and administrator of the eternal counsels of God, of the purpose of God from eternity, and, coming like that, He imposes (I trust that it is not the wrong word to use) the purpose of God upon the vessel. He gathers the vessel into the purpose in a sovereign way. It is as though He circled around and took charge of the vessel in an outward way and said, 'This is the vessel of the eternal purpose of God.' He takes charge of it, comes 'upon' for that.

But then He entered 'in' also, and they were filled, and this had a further meaning. It meant this, that the inward life of the vessel must correspond to the outward purpose. That is tremendous. You see, the old dispensation was not like that, and this is the problem that the prophets were dealing with all the time. The outward form was there. Israel had their temple, they were offering their sacrifices, they were going through all the ritual, but their inward life was far from corresponding to that. God had to say, through the prophets, 'Away with your sacrifices, I do not want them!' (cf. Isaiah i. 10-14). The Lord Jesus took that up. "Sacrifice and offering thou wouldest not, but a body didst thou prepare for me; in whole burnt offerings and sacrifices for sin thou hadst no pleasure; then said I, Lo, I am come (in the roll of the book it is written of me) to do thy will, O God" (Hebrews x. 5-7).

Formalism never does the will of God; merely external system, however much it corresponds to the technique of the letter, never does the will of God; and the Holy Ghost was having none of that. He did not come in sovereignty to take up a lot of new people in a new dispensation, and give them forms and order, and make them do things in such and such a manner, merely in an outward way. He was going to have the inner life of the Church corresponding to the purpose. You find before long that He very severely comes upon anything that does not correspond. Ananias and Sapphira will know you cannot carry on in an outward way, pretending all is right. The Holy Ghost has seen inside the contradiction, and is not allowing it to pass.

Many want the coming 'upon' because they want to feel the power, feel themselves taken up, manipulated and moved. There has been a great deal of that sort of thing, which has not carried with it an inward correspondence. But the Lord's end can never be reached fully while there is any lack of true consistency between the purpose of God and the life of the people called to that purpose. "I...beseech you to walk worthily of the calling wherewith ye were called" (Ephesians iv. 1). Oh, I do beg of you to have continuous dealings with God on this matter of the indwelling Spirit—not just for purposes of service, or power, but for purposes of life.

One of the tragedies of many Christians and many servants of God is this, that they can believe and give expression to things which are positively false, and propagate those things and do harm to other Christians by propagating them, and yet the Holy Ghost never seems to be able to make them aware that they are not telling the truth. I do not mean in Bible teaching, but in relation to other servants of God, and other work that

God is doing. The solemn fact that there are such prejudices, suspicions, criticisms, misrepresentations, and so on, ought to drive us to the Lord with earnest appeal—'Oh, Lord, it is no good my being engaged in Thy work, doing a lot of things for Thee, being prominent among men, perhaps, and well known for my Christian service, if yet, after all, the Holy Ghost cannot correct me within, put me right, give me a bad time when I say something not true. Save me from saying anything that does not correspond with the truth, or of which my inward life is a contradiction.' The Spirit within is to adjust us to the purpose of God. If we habitually, constantly, fall into ways which are not according to the Spirit, so that we become known for that kind of unpleasantness, we had better ask the Holy Spirit to do a deeper work in us. It is no use our having the deep things of God, while people know us as most difficult to get on with, always making life unpleasant for others. It will not do; it is a contradiction of the indwelling Spirit. He does not want us to have the system of things merely outwardly. We must have the inner life to correspond.

So we see that He came 'upon' to possess for the purpose of God, and He came 'within' to see that everything in the inner life corresponded to that purpose.

CHAPTER EIGHT

THE CRY OF THE PROPHETS FOR HOLINESS

"For they that dwell in Jerusalem, and their rulers, because they knew him not, nor the voices of the prophets which are read every sabbath, fulfilled them by condemning him" (Acts xiii. 27).

W E WERE TAKING NOTE, in our last chapter, of a contrast which is marked between the old dispensation and the new: of how much there is to be missed if there is a continuing in the fixed order of the old, and how much there is to be gained by moving into the essential nature of the new. This is found focused for us in the passage we have read.

Without repeating too much of our previous meditation, may I just say that it is perfectly clear in the New Testament, from the Book of the Acts onwards, that the people in the new dispensation, the dispensation of the Holy Ghost, were required to keep completely free from everything set, from everything of a conclusive position, *excepting fundamental facts of the faith*. So far as their mentality was concerned—yes, their religious, traditional mentality, the mentality which had been formed by their very birth into Israel, by all that they had received through training and teaching from their infancy upward, they were to be always open to the Lord even for the revolutionary. They were called upon to come into a place where that no longer held them, but where the Lord was perfectly free to do the revolutionary thing in them and make them revise all their thinking—in the light, not of anything contradictory, but of God's fuller meaning in all that they they knew of the Word of God; where they acknowledged that the Lord really had 'more light and truth to break forth from His Word'—indeed, so much more as to make all that they already knew seem as nothing.

You find, therefore, that this necessity precipitated crises in their spiritual course, and sometimes brought them to a standstill, where a tremendous conflict was set up; but the Holy Spirit was sufficiently in possession to win, and to be able to carry them further. That happened with Peter, on the housetop at Joppa. It happened with Saul of Tarsus. There is no doubt about it that, in acting as he did, Saul was acting upon the basis of the Old Testament Scriptures. He thought he had the full support of the Word of God for what he was doing. When he met Jesus of Nazareth out from heaven as he went to Damascus, although he capitulated there and then and acknowledged Jesus as his Lord, his great problem was, 'How am I going to reconcile my Old Testament with this?' He went away into Arabia, and probably for two years he was occupied there with the reconciliation of the Old Testament with the fact of Jesus as Christ and Lord. And he got well through, came back from his desert, and, caught in the resistless stream of the Spirit, became a mighty servant of God.

We want to go on a little further now. We are saying that here, in this new dispensation as represented in the Book of the Acts, the prophets are being re-interpreted, or their inner meaning is being brought to light, with all that that inner meaning implies. We know that the inauguration of the dispensation on the day of Pentecost was accompanied by a quoting of the prophets. It began with Joel—"This is that which hath been spoken through the prophet Joel" (Acts ii. 16)—and went on with other Old Testament quotations pointing to that time. Now, either by direct citation or fulfilment (as clearly seen in the case of the Joel prophecy) or by an unmistakable implication, the prophets are here brought in in many connections.

CHRIST ALONE THE MEASURE
OF WHAT IS OF GOD

You pass from chapter ii of the Book of the Acts, and go on to chapter v, the very terrible, dark story of Ananias and Sapphira. Where did the prophets come in in that?

In the first chapter of the Book of Ezekiel, you have what was introduced spiritually on the day of Pentecost. There you have that wonderful, though difficult, vision of the living creatures, the wheels full of eyes, the Spirit in the wheels, the Spirit of life going, always going: the Spirit, life, eyes, and the irresistible movement from heaven in relation to the Man upon the throne. "Acts" begins there. The Lord Jesus was received up, out of this world; and in relation to that Man in the throne there is this going on here, touching the earth and yet detached from it; touching, but not fixed here; a heavenly thing. And that is moving with tremendous directness and deliberation. That is like the second chapter of "Acts." The Man in the throne; the wheels, the eternal counsels of God, the goings of God from eternity; the living creatures, the Church; the life within, the Spirit of life there, with His perfect vision—"full of eyes." Is that not what is here?

Yes; but that is the beginning of "Ezekiel." At the other end of his prophecy you have this—away, up from the earth—a vision, a picture, of a temple, a spiritual house, very fully depicted and defined, with every detail marked. The man who leads the prophet round goes measuring, measuring, giving the measure of every detail. This house is all of the Holy Ghost. It is all a measure of Christ, in every part. This thing is not on the earth; it is heavenly measurement. Before you can have the river issuing from the sanctuary, flowing on in increasing volume, deepening and widening, making everything on its banks to live, and swallowing up death in victory as it proceeds, you have to have the house utterly according to God; and then the one overall statement about it is: "the whole limit thereof round about shall be most holy" (Ezekiel xliv. 12). It is all of God; it is all of Christ, His risen, exalted Son. It is out from Him, through a Church constituted on a heavenly pattern, that the life flows; and it is flowing here in "Acts."

HOLINESS THE LAW OF WHAT IS OF GOD

Now Ananias and his wife violate the very governing law of that house—holiness; and what happens? That is where Israel failed to hear the voices of the prophets. We said, in our previous meditation, that they carried on the external formalities of the temple, the daily services, the ritual and the liturgy, adopted the forms and the vestments, but the inner life did not correspond. It was the cry of the prophets that a system was being maintained and preserved out of relation to the inner life of the people. The prophets throughout are crying for holiness. The trouble lay there. And what does this matter of holiness really mean? When you really get to the heart of it, what is it? "Why hath Satan filled thy heart to lie to the Holy Spirit?" (Acts v. 3). That is unholiness. The act of Ananias and Sapphira implies something deeper—that sinister mind behind; Satan finding an opportunity of getting into these holy precincts, this heavenly realm, corrupting and polluting, and establishing his lie. "He is a liar, and the father thereof," said the Lord (John viii. 44). A lie right in the presence of the Holy Ghost! The life of the Spirit and the Spirit of life do not just go on ignoring conditions. They require that first of all everything shall be constituted on God's heavenly pattern; that is only saying, constituted on the pattern of Christ His Son; that it shall be really an expression and representation of the Lord Jesus by the Holy Spirit.

THE SPIRIT SPONTANEOUSLY REPRODUCES THE NATURE OF CHRIST

Now, I am not going back behind what I said earlier. I am not saying that we must take the Bible in its letter and phrases and make a mould, a scriptural mould, which we think is the New Testament order. That is not the point at all. Development did not come about in the beginning in that way. Every fresh reproduction of the Church, in any part of the Roman Empire or beyond, in the days of the Apostles, came about, not by taking thither a fixed mould and trying to pour people into that mould and to reproduce the shape of things that existed somewhere else. It began with life—life from heaven—"the Holy Ghost sent forth from heaven" (I Peter i. 12). And wherever the believers went, two things were imperative: firstly, baptism, as a testimony to the fact that an old order was finished, and that everything now had to have as new a beginning as anybody must have who has died and been buried; and secondly, the gift of the Holy Ghost, the Spirit of life, coming to take up residence within those concerned. When the Holy Spirit comes in and has His way, He relieves you of all the responsibility of New Testament order; you have no more burden and responsibility about that than a tree has in producing leaves and fruit. No tree ever spends hours and hours worrying and fretting, 'How can I bring forth some leaves? How can I develop my fruit?' It just lives—it yields to the life process; and the rest happens. That was the glorious spontaneity of New Testament churches—they just came about. And the Lord must have them like that—constituted from heaven by the Holy Ghost; not man bringing his form of church and church government, his mould, his conception of things, and saying, 'This is our conception of a Bible church.' No, it is the product of life. As that Spirit of life was allowed to work, things took a certain course and a certain form, and that was the form of Christ. The Holy Spirit took responsibility. "I will build My church," the Lord Jesus had said (Matthew xvi. 18), and He meant it; and He is found doing it here.

THE NATURE OF CHRIST IS UTTER HOLINESS

But remember: Christ, in the innermost expression of what He is, is very holy. "The holy thing which is begotten" said the angel to Mary, "shall be called the Son of God" (Luke i. 35, A.R.V.). He "offered himself without blemish unto God" (Hebrews ix. 14). He was "...in all points tempted like as we are, yet without sin" (Heb. iv. 15). Christ was and is without sin. He is infinitely holy. The great antagonist of Christ, that unholy one, is always seeking to destroy what is of Christ, by introducing a contradiction, a lie, giving the lie to the holiness of Christ; and that is what happened here.

I do feel that this is a very solemn matter for us all. I have not said this without a very great deal of exercise in my own heart. It is not an easy thing to say. Some of us are not ignorant of Satan's devices. Who has a right to talk about holiness? Who is sufficient in holiness to talk to other people about it? Holiness is what Christ is. Who of us could say we are like that?

THE SPIRIT ARRESTED BY CONSCIOUS UNHOLINESS

Unholiness is that which is not consistent with Christ. It is the opposite of what Christ is; it is a contradiction of Christ. The mighty purpose of God, the mighty course of the Spirit of God—all that has come in with this dispensation—can be suddenly brought under arrest, and a tragedy occur, if you or I knowingly dabble with unholiness. "His wife also being privy to it" (Acts v. 2) means that this was conscious. I am not speaking of the unholiness which is ours in general—though we are not going to condone or make light of it. What I am speaking about now is deliberate sin in the very presence of the Holy Spirit. Ananias and Sapphira deliberately planned to give to the Lord only a part of the proceeds of their sale, but to represent it as being the whole. If they had been really in the good of the régime of the Holy Spirit, they would have known the Spirit saying to them: 'That is not right—it is a contradiction of Christ.' And may we not confidently conclude that the Holy Spirit did warn them? Were there not two voices which, though perhaps not audible, yet spoke in them, the one warning from evil, the other suggesting this deceit, the voice of the Spirit and the voice of Satan? They were disposed to listen to the tempter's voice, and Satan 'filled their hearts.' That is the kind of unholiness we are speaking about.

We are in the dispensation of the Spirit. If we are really in the good of this dispensation, that is, if the Holy Spirit is in us, He will tell us—He does tell us. If we will, we can know the mind of the Spirit on all issues of right and wrong. But until we yield to the Spirit, everything is in suspense. The whole life of the Spirit is brought under arrest. The Lord was very positive in laying down the principles for the dispensation. He left us in no doubt as to what His attitude is toward this sort of thing. If He does not act in the same way every time, and if we do not fall down dead, it does not mean that something just as tragic does not take place in us. The Spirit is arrested, and spiritual death comes in, and there is no going on from that time. There is a sense in which, spiritually, we also are 'carried out.'

Yes, this is a solemn matter. Forgive me if I seem to be oppressive, but this matter of holiness is so very pertinent, and so very much bound up with all that we are seeking to see—all the wonderful meaning of the Spirit's being here and of His being able to go right on; life and fulness, growing depth, increasing vitality, ever fuller knowledge, the swallowing up of death in victory. That is to be the spiritual existence of the Church, but that can all be arrested by some unholiness, known to be such and not dealt with before God, repudiated and refused. Whatever that may mean to you in its particular application, remember that it is a very dangerous thing to have an unsettled controversy with the Holy Ghost—dangerous not only for you, but perhaps for many others who will be affected.

THE PERIL OF PERSISTING IN UNHOLINESS

Oh, the tragedy of a controversy with the Lord not cleared up! Surely, seeing the setting of a matter like this, we must face the specific things from the standpoint of the great background. You have not an adequate motive for dealing with particular points of outstanding unholiness unless you see this whole matter in its great setting. If it is merely something personal, relating only to us, we may or we may not feel it is worth clearing up. But look! The whole course of God's eternal counsels, coming down our way and gathering us in: the mighty purpose of God to be realised in and through us: the far-reaching range of those purposes of God which would find us as their vehicle and channel: all that God would do of making Himself known to us for the sake of others; all brought under arrest because of that! Yes, a personal ministry, a great ministry which might be very far-reaching, may all be set aside—the Lord, in keeping with His own nature, would have to set it aside—if there were a persistence in something about which He had spoken but which was not dealt with. It is a tremendous background.

The psalmist said: "I know, O Lord, that thy judgments are righteous, and that in faithfulness thou hast afflicted me" (Psalms cxix. 75). What did he mean? Evidently he had gone through some severe handling by the Lord, and as he looked at what his wrong involved for the Lord's people—how many were affected and how it touched the Lord's honour—he said: 'Only the faithfulness of God lies behind His dealing with me: He has to be faithful to Himself and faithful to me, and not let me off; and He has to be faithful to His own nature, His own righteousness, because so much is bound up with it.' May the Lord show us just what that means, and give us grace. Oh, we need protecting, we need safeguarding in this matter of a holy walk with God; we need to clear up every controversy with Him because there is so much bound up with it.

We see that those that dwelt in Jerusalem, and their rulers and those whom they represented, would not clear up the controversy which God had with them, and they were set aside, and another nation bringing forth the fruits of the Kingdom was brought in. What a loss! And do you think that the Lord will deal with us differently? It may not be our salvation that will go, but surely our vocation is of some consequence! The Lord give us grace!

CHAPTER NINE

A RECAPITULATION

W E HAVE BEEN SEEING that in the dispensation of the Old Testament the Holy Spirit was operating as the Spirit of prophecy, making everything a prophecy. He was causing everything within the Divine economy to point onward, to imply something further, which was not clear to those who lived in those times and who were most closely connected with what was being done and said; and that comprehensive work of the Holy Spirit through those ages was all heading up to what would be the nature, character and purpose of the dispensation in which we live. This dispensation is marked by two outstanding features—two aspects of one thing. It is the dispensation, firstly, of Christ enthroned at the right hand of the Majesty in the heavens, and secondly, of the Holy Spirit here within the Church to make good all that that means. That prophetic activity was many-sided; that is, it pointed to various characteristics of the age which lay ahead; and we have been looking at some of those characteristics in the foregoing chapters.

So that now we start here. We have come to and are living in the dispensation of the spiritual fulfilment of what the prophets foretold; but that fulfilment is not merely and only objective, as in the history of the world or of the Church, in an outward way. That fulfilment is an inward thing, and moreover an inward thing so far as every member of Christ is concerned. It is something which must come down to the youngest. Please do not think that this is for older or more advanced Christians! It involves every one of us equally.

SPIRITUAL VISION

The first thing that the prophets were occupied with, and which has its fulfillment in an inward way in the members of Christ in this dispensation, is spiritual vision. Everything in the purpose of God, for its fulfilment and for our attainment unto it, rests firstly upon this—that the Holy Spirit has become to us the Spirit of revelation, and has made us to see, in its grand outline, what God is after. The details are filled in as we go on.

(a) THE FACULTY OF SEEING

That has two sides. First of all, there is the faculty of seeing. The prophets had much to say about this. You know that, because of a certain prejudice on the part of the people of Israel, by which they were not disposed to see what God wanted them to see (because they had their own visions and ideas and were not ready for what God wanted), a double judgment was passed upon them, and the Lord closed their eyes. The word was given to Isaiah for this people: "Go, and tell this people, Hear ye indeed, but understand not; and see ye indeed, but perceive not. Make the heart of this people fat, and make their ears heavy, and shut their eyes" (Isaiah vi. 9, 10). That was a judgment, and a terrible one: the very faculty of spiritual sight, of vision, was neutralised. It was a terrible judgment, with terrible consequences; for, as we have seen, the ultimate consequence was that they lost all that God intended, and that was no small thing. It passed away from them. It was given to another nation—a heavenly nation. It is a terrible judgment to have a faculty of spiritual sight nullified; and if that is so, it must be a very great thing in the desire and grace and lovingkindness of the Lord that people should have such vision, such sight.

The faculty for seeing is a birthright of every child of God. Do not think that you have to live the Christian life for a long time, receive more teaching, and reach a certain advanced position, before you begin to see. It is a part of your very new birth. The Lord said to Nicodemus: "Except one be born anew, he cannot *see* the kingdom of God" (John iii. 3). By implication He said, 'When you are born from above, you will see.' The commission to the Apostle Paul was: "...unto whom I send thee, to open their eyes" (Acts xxvi. 17, 18). The very symbolical work of the Lord Jesus in the days of His flesh, in opening the eyes of the blind, was pointing on to what was going to happen when He went above and the Holy Spirit came, and men saw. It is a part of your new birth to see. I am not saying that you will see all at once, that you will see all that those who have gone far on with the Lord are seeing; but the faculty of sight has been given to you. Are you using it? Do you know that it is just as true of your spiritual life as it is of your physical—that you have spiritual eyes, and that they have been opened? If not, get right down to the Lord about this, because something is wrong.

> **There must be a faculty for seeing before there can be an object seen.**

(b) THE OBJECT SEEN

And not only the faculty, but the object, of sight; it is a part of the vision. There must be a faculty for seeing before there can be an object seen, but, having the faculty, you must have an object to see; and the object is—what? What was the thing that came to the perception, the recognition of people, when the Holy Ghost came? What did they begin to see? They began to see the significance of Jesus Christ, and there is one very familiar phrase which indicates what that is—"the eternal purpose." They are one and the same thing—the significance of Christ, and God's eternal purpose. The purpose of God from eternity is concerning His Son—the place that His Son holds in the very universe according to God's mind; the tremendous comprehensiveness of Christ; the tremendous implications of the very being and existence of Christ; the tremendous consequences that are bound up with Jesus Christ. They did not see it all at once, but they began to see the Lord Jesus. They began to see that this was not just a man among men, not just the man of Galilee. No, He is infinitely greater than that, overwhelming. This mighty impact of a meaning about Jesus Christ is too big to hold, so great that you cannot grasp it. It is overwhelming and devastating. They began to see *that*; that was their vision. Out of that vision everything else came. Look at them and hear them, recognise what a new and great Christ they have found, what a significant Christ He is, how everything is bound up with Him. All destiny is centred in Him; He is the only consequence.

The prophets had dimly seen something. You will hear a prophet saying: "His name shall be called Wonderful, Counsellor, Mighty God, Everlasting Father, Prince of Peace" (Isaiah ix. 6). Well, that prophet had begun to see something; and there are other things like that. It is but a beginning, but what they are saying is that this One is going to come into full view. 'We are pointing on to Him,' they say, 'looking on to the day when this One shall come right out into recognition.' And this is that day; we are in the day of the prophets' fulfilled vision.

These are not merely words, great ideas. It has to be true of you, even though it may be only at its beginnings, that the apprehension of Jesus Christ in your heart is tremendous, is overwhelming. He is your vision, and He has mastered you in the sense of His greatness. We shall never get through without vision. We shall break if we have no vision, or if our vision is arrested. If something interferes with the clearness, the fulness, of our vision, we shall begin to go around in circles, not knowing where we are. The vision will carry us on if it is kept clear and full. Have you got it? When the Holy Spirit came on the day of Pentecost, this tremendous thing happened—they saw the Lord, and in seeing Him they began to be emancipated from everything that was other or less than He. Those who did not see, well, they began to pass out and either became nonentities in the spiritual realm or, because of their prejudices, enemies to those who saw. The instance in John ix was fulfilled in a spiritual sense. The Lord opened the eyes of the man born blind. What happened? The others cast him out. Those who saw in the day of the Spirit's coming were excommunicated by many who were prejudiced. They were cut off. There is always a price attached to seeing. But that is not our subject now. Simply, what the Lord has been saying to us, in the first place, is that He desires to have, and must have—and therefore He can have—in this dispensation a people with their eyes open, a seeing people who have the faculty in themselves.

(c) VISION TO BE PERSONAL AND INCREASING IN EVERY BELIEVER

Now, the difference between the dispensations is just that. In the old dispensation everything had to be told to the people. They had to get it secondhand from someone else; it was never their own, it was not original. In the new dispensation of the Holy Spirit, the thing was in themselves; the root of the matter was in them. But Christianity has become very largely a system which has reverted to the level of the old dispensation. That is, so many Christians have their lives based upon addresses and sermons and going to meetings and being told by other people. How many Christians do you find to-day who are really living in the good of a throbbing, personal revelation of Jesus Christ? I do not think that is an improper question. The great need of our day is for the people of God to be re-established on the basis upon which the Church was founded in the beginning, a Holy Ghost basis; and the very beginning of that basis is this—not to have a lot of information given to Christians, but that the Christians should have the faculty of spiritual sight within them, should have the capacity for seeing, and should themselves be seeing. Can you say: 'My eyes are open; I am seeing God's eternal purpose, I am seeing the significance of Christ; I am seeing more and more as to the Lord Jesus'? Unless it is like that, we shall leave the Holy Ghost behind, and we shall have to turn round and go back to find Him where we left Him, because a life in the Holy Ghost right up to date is a life of continually increasing vision. Vision is absolutely essential, both as to faculty and as to object.

THE INSTRUMENTALITY OF THE CROSS
(a) DEATH, THE REMOVAL OF WHAT IS OF MAN

Still recapitulating, we went on next to see that, in order to keep the faculty alive and the vision growing, the Holy Spirit has an instrument. He always works by an instrument, and that instrument is the Cross; that is, the principle of the Cross of the Lord Jesus.

This means, on the one side, the removal of everything that cannot come into the new Kingdom; getting rid of that which in God's sight is dead and has to be put away—that is to say, the sum total of the self-life. Call it by other names if you like—the flesh, the natural life, the old Adam, and so on. I prefer this designation—the self-principle—because it is very comprehensive: whether it be the self- principle acting in the outward direction, in assertiveness, in imposition, where the self is the impact; or whether it act in the inward direction, drawing to self. Oh, how many aspects there are of the self-life in both these directions! We may know some of the more obvious ones, but are we not learning how deeply root-ed, with countless fibres, is this self? We never get to the end of it. It spreads its tentacles throughout our whole constitution—'I,' somehow, strong or weak. It is just as bad for it to be weak as to be strong. Self-pity is only a way of drawing attention to ourselves and being occupied with ourselves, and it is just as pernicious as self-assertiveness. It is *self*, all the same; it belongs to the same root, it comes from the same source. It all comes from that false life of the one who said: "I will ascend into heaven, I will exalt my throne above the stars of God; and I will sit upon the mount of congregation...I will ascend above the heights of the clouds; I will make myself like the Most High" (Isaiah xiv. 13, 14). 'I'—'I'—'I'—. Truly, we cannot exhaust the forms of this self-life. Now, because it is so many-sided and so far-reaching and so deeply rooted, the Lord cannot deal with it all at once in the active way. He has dealt with it all at once potentially in the Cross of His Son. But now the application of that must go on. You and I must know continually the application of the principle of the Cross to the various forms of the self-life. We must learn both the need for and the manner of its being smitten, stricken, laid low and brought under the hand of God; and that is the meaning of 'disciple,' that is the meaning of training. It is on that side of things that the Holy Ghost is constantly taking precautions against the self-life. Even in the case of a far-advanced and well-crucified Apostle, it becomes necessary, in the presence of great Divine deposits, for God to take precautions and put a stake in his flesh and give him a messenger of Satan to buffet him, lest he should become exalted (II Corinthians xii. 7). That is very practical. The Holy Ghost uses the principle and the law of the Cross repeatedly and ever more deeply in order to get rid of the rubbish—that which occupies the ground which must be occupied by the Lord Himself. There has to be a lot of clearing of the ground in order to build the new spiritual kingdom within.

(b) RESURRECTION—THE EXPRESSION OF THE LORD HIMSELF

So, on the other side, the corresponding thing is the power of His resurrection, which can never be known except as we know the power of His Cross; and it is in knowing Him and the power of His resurrection that our education on the positive side is found. Oh, to know Him and the power of His resurrection! It is a wonderful thing when you and I are brought to the place where on the side of nature—and not feignedly, but very utterly—we are compelled to recognise the awful and terrible reality: 'This is an end of everything. I who have said so much, I who have preached so much, I who have taught so much, I who have done so much—I am at an end.' It is the sentence of death; no more is possible; and it is terribly and grimly real. And then God raises the dead! You go on, and there is something more of the Lord than there was before. It is a great thing to see how God does raise the dead again and again. The same person is alive again, and there is more than there ever was, because there has been a greater emptiness than there ever was. It is a very safe position from the Lord's standpoint.

What are we learning, what is the meaning of that way, what is it we are inheriting along the line of such experiences? Just this—we are knowing the Lord, that is all. We are knowing this, that everything is of the Lord, and whatever is not of Him is nothing at all. It must be of the Lord or there is no more possibility, no hope. We are the most ready to say, 'If it depends upon me, there is nothing more possible'; and then the Lord does it. You see what He is doing by the death side of the Cross. He is clearing ground for Himself, and then He is occupying the ground; He is building Himself up as the risen Lord on the ground which has been purged of our old self. The Holy Spirit uses the Cross to keep the way open, to keep the vision clear and growing.

A NEW LIBERTY

Further, we pointed out that when the dispensation changed on the day of Pentecost, from that moment there was a marvellous emancipation into a new liberty. In the old dispensation the whole order was one of bondage, of thraldom; people were in a strait-jacket of a religious system. In the new dispensation, the strait-jacket has gone. There is nothing that suggests a strait-jacket in the Book of the Acts. People are out, they are free. There will still be some things to be taken away, like Peter's remnant of tradition in the presence of the call to the house of Cornelius, and so on. But in the main they are out, released, and it is the Holy Spirit who brings that about and demands that it shall be maintained.

The Lord wants and needs such a people to-day, just as then. First-ly, a people of vision; and then, secondly, a thoroughly crucified people, giving the Lord full scope for all His purpose—a people who, in them-selves, have been removed out of the Lord's way. (That is the meaning of the Book of the Acts—that people are out of the Lord's way, and He can move freely.) Then, the Holy Ghost, having effected this liberation, demands that it shall be preserved. We were pointing out earlier that the constant and persistent tendency of man and effort of the enemy is to bring back again into a yoke of bondage, imprisoning the Holy Ghost in some set, crystallized system of things—a Church system, an ecclesiastical system, a man-made religious order, a formality, an organization, and all such things as so often commence with a Divine idea, and then take charge of the Divine idea and make it to serve them instead of everything serving it.

That is the peril, and the Holy Ghost will have none of it. He can only go as far as He has liberty to go. He demands that we be out in a free place with Him; He demands His own rights as the Spirit of liberty. He will be hampered by nothing. If we try to hamper Him, to put chains on Him, we shall lose His values. He demands that we shall never allow ourselves to be brought into any fixed form or economy or limit of any kind; that we shall be God's free people. That is not licence. That does not give the individual the right to be a free-lance, nor mean that we can go and do everything that our impulse would suggest, and independently snap our fingers at all spiritual authority. It never meant that. But it does mean that the Lord will not allow us to crystallize His things and put them into a box and say, 'That is the limit.' He demands that we should be ready always to receive and respond to new light. If His new light demands that we make new adjustments—revolutionary adjustments sometimes—we are to be so free in the Lord that we can do it. It is most necessary that we should be like that, as God's free people. It is a very blessed thing to have the expanse of the universe in which to move.

HOLINESS THE CHARACTER
OF THE NEW DISPENSATION

Now our next point was that the whole nature of things, characteristic of the dispensation of the Holy Spirit and of all the Spirit's movements, is holiness—that everything shall inwardly correspond to what is outward. Progress can be brought to an abrupt standstill; all this movement of the Spirit of God can be suddenly arrested; there may be an end beyond which there is no advance, if there is some debatable thing between the Holy Ghost and us. We have to keep very short accounts with the Holy Spirit on all matters of question, and He is resident in us for this purpose. Why are there so many things in Christians that are not as the Lord would have them? It is simply because those concerned have not recognised and taken to heart this—that the Holy Spirit is their personal, indwelling Teacher, and they have to listen to Him. How much is lost because of that failure! 'Oh, there is a meeting: I do not think I will go to it—I will go for a walk.' So off you go. In that meeting was the very word God meant you to have! If only you had said, 'I would like to go for a walk, but there is a meeting; I will ask the Lord whether He wants me there.' Something has been lost that you may not recover for yourself, because you failed to ask the Lord.

And so in a thousand different ways. If only we listened to the Holy Spirit, we should make more progress. He talks to us about all sorts of practical matters. For example, we need to be taught by the Spirit in the matter of our merriment—how to be merry without being frivolous, and how to be serious without being long-faced and miserable. We are not going to giggle our way through life, but at the same time the Lord does not want us to be poor, solemn creatures. He does want us to be serious people, but do not think that solemnity is necessarily spiritual life. I read in my morning paper of a poor girl in Australia, who was overtaken of a certain disease which deprived her of the ability to smile. She was brought by air to have an operation in London—and after the operation she could smile! I think a lot of Christians need that operation!

But in this whole matter we have to know the discipline of the Holy Spirit, because spiritual value, spiritual increase, is bound up with it. In matters of holiness, and controversies with the Lord—which may come down to very small points, such as details of dress, the wearing of adornments, and so on—it is remarkable how adjustments are made by many young Christians on these practical matters without anything being said to them by anyone. Who told them to do it? No one; but they came to feel that the Lord would have them do it, that is all. Such people are going on; they are beginning to count for God. I take those points, not to impose law upon you, but to show the principle of the Holy Spirit's being able to speak to us inside on matters where the Lord may not be fully in agreement, and, as He speaks and we respond, we go on. The Holy Spirit adds and adds.

SPIRIT-DIRECTED SERVICE: NO EXCLUSIVISM

As you come into the Book of the Acts further, you find that the Holy Spirit was the Spirit of service. You get to chapter viii, and the movement out from Jerusalem is absolutely spontaneous. Philip goes down to Samaria. Who told him he should go to Samaria? Surely we may say that the Holy Spirit led him there. They moved out under the sovereign control of the Holy Spirit. He was the Spirit of service; He brought it about. And when you come to chapter x, oh, what a blessed aspect of that development! We find it in keeping with what the prophets, though imperfectly, were made to see. In chapter x the Holy Spirit precipitates the whole matter of going beyond the bounds of Israel out to the Gentiles. How do the prophets come into that? Well, what about Jonah? It is a terrible story, that story in the little book of Jonah. It is not the whole life and work of Jonah, but it is practically all that most people know about him—that he had a fierce quarrel with the Lord. "Doest thou well to be angry?...I do well to be angry" (Jonah iv. 9). Think of a man answering God like that! Why? Because the large-hearted grace of God had said, in effect, 'There must be no exclusivism; I am not bound up wholly and solely with Israel; my heart embraces the heathen as well; the whole world is the scope of My grace.' Jonah was so exclusive—there could be nothing beyond his own circle, and he came into controversy with the Lord.

The Lord has scattered here and there through His Word lessons and illustrations which emphasize that. What about Ruth? She is a Moabitess, a heathen, outside the pale of Israel. It is the most beautiful romance in the Bible, that little story of Ruth. What is the Lord saying? Look at the genealogy of the Lord Jesus, and you will find Ruth, the Moabitess there. But if that is impressive, what about Rahab the harlot, the resident in doomed Jericho, who had faith and expressed it by the scarlet cord in the window? And in the genealogy of Jesus Christ, Rahab the harlot has a place. What is God saying? He takes up in the new dispensation the principle of that prophetic work of the Holy Spirit through the Old Testament. In Acts x He precipitates it, as if to say, 'Go out to all; let there be no exclusivism.' It is impossible to be people governed by the Holy Spirit and not to have the world in your heart—not to be concerned for all the Lord's people, and for all who are not the Lord's people. He will precipitate that issue. Let us allow that truth to search us deeply.

The point of all that we have been saying is this: that when the Holy Spirit comes and really has His way, all these things are spontaneous;

they happen: these are the features of His government. Oh, that the Lord might recover a people like that, free from all set, ecclesiastical, religious, traditional limits and bounds—a people in the Spirit. The Lord make us every one to be of that kind.

NOTES

PROPHETIC MINISTRY

PROPHETIC MINISTRY

PROPHETIC MINISTRY

PROPHETIC MINISTRY

Destiny Image titles
you will enjoy reading

THE COSTLY ANOINTING
by Lori Wilke.
In this book, teacher and prophetic songwriter Lori Wilke boldly reveals God's requirements for being entrusted with an awesome power and authority. She speaks directly from God's heart to your heart concerning the most costly anointing. This is a word that will change your life!
ISBN 1-56043-051-6

A HEART FOR GOD
by Charles P. Schmitt.
This powerful book will send you on a 31-day journey with David from brokenness to wholeness. Few men come to God with as many millstones around their necks as David did. Nevertheless, David pressed beyond adversity, sin, and failure into the very forgiveness and deliverance of God. The life of David will bring hope to those bound by generational curses, those born in sin, and those raised in shame. David's life will inspire faith in the hearts of the dysfunctional, the failure-ridden, and the fallen!
ISBN 1-56043-157-1

REQUIREMENTS FOR GREATNESS
by Lori Wilke.
Everyone longs for greatness, but do we know what God's requirements are? In this life-changing message, Lori Wilke shows how Jesus exemplified true greatness, and how we must take on His attributes of justice, mercy, and humility to attain that greatness in His Kingdom.
ISBN 1-56043-152-0

THE ASCENDED LIFE
by Bernita J. Conway.
A believer does not need to wait until Heaven to experience an intimate relationship with the Lord. When you are born again, your life becomes His, and He pours His life into yours. Here Bernita Conway explains from personal study and experience the truth of "abiding in the Vine," the Lord Jesus Christ. When you grasp this understanding and begin to walk in it, it will change your whole life and relationship with your heavenly Father!
ISBN 1-56043-337-X

Available at your local Christian bookstore.

For more information and sample chapters, visit www.reapernet.com

Exciting titles
by Bill Hamon

➤ APOSTLES, PROPHETS AND THE COMING MOVES OF GOD
Author of the "Prophets" series, Dr. Bill Hamon brings the same anointed instruction in this new series on apostles! Learn about the apostolic age and how apostles and prophets work together. Find out God's end-time plans for the Church!
ISBN 0-939868-09-1

➤ PROPHETS AND PERSONAL PROPHECY
This book defines the role of a prophet or prophetess and gives the reader strategic guidelines for judging prophecy. Many of the stories included are taken from Dr. Bill's ministry and add that "hands on" practicality that is quickly making this book a best-seller.
ISBN 0-939868-03-2

➤ PROPHETS AND THE PROPHETIC MOVEMENT
This sequel to *Prophets and Personal Prophecy* is packed with the same kind of cutting instruction that made the first volume a best-seller. Prophetic insights, how-to's, and warnings make this book essential for the Spirit-filled church.
ISBN 0-939868-04-0

➤ PROPHETS, PITFALLS, AND PRINCIPLES
This book shows you how to recognize your hidden "root" problems, and detect and correct character flaws and "weed seed" attitudes. It also can teach you how to discern true prophets using Dr. Hamon's ten M's.
ISBN 0-939868-05-9

Available at your local Christian bookstore.

For more information and sample chapters, visit www.reapernet.com

Destiny Image titles
you will enjoy reading

▬ RESTORING THE HOUSE OF GOD
by Frank M. Reid, III.
Our only hope of reconnecting with our Lord and the culture around us is to return to the Lord Himself. He will build His own Church, with much less help from us than we realize. This book shows the power of restoring the Church by restoring the intimacy of relationship with our Lord and then with the people God has put into our lives.
ISBN 1-56043-349-3

▬ FATHER, FORGIVE US!
by Jim W. Goll.
What is holding back a worldwide "great awakening"? What hinders the Church all over the world from rising up and bringing in the greatest harvest ever known? The answer is simple: sin! God is calling Christians today to take up the mantle of identificational intercession and repent for the sins of the present and past; for the sins of our fathers; for the sins of the nations. Will you heed the call? This book shows you how!
ISBN 0-7684-2025-3

▬ FLOODS UPON DRY GROUND
by Charles P. Schmitt.
Do you really know the history of the Church through the ages? This book may surprise you! Charles P. Schmitt, pastor of Immanuel's Church in the Washington D.C. area, gives an inspiring and thought-provoking history of the Church from a charismatic perspective. History is not finished yet, and neither is God! Redis-cover your roots and learn how the current rivers of renewal and revival fit into God's great plan for this world.
ISBN 0-7684-2012-1

▬ DIGGING THE WELLS OF REVIVAL
by Lou Engle.
Did you know that just beneath your feet are deep wells of revival? God is call-ing us today to unstop the wells and reclaim the spiritual inheritance of our nation, declares Lou Engle. As part of the pastoral staff at Harvest Rock Church and founder of its "24-Hour House of Prayer," he has experienced firsthand the impor-tance of knowing and praying over our spiritual heritage. Let's renew covenant with God, reclaim our glorious roots, and believe for the greatest revival the world has ever known!
ISBN 0-7684-2015-6

Available at your local Christian bookstore.

Destiny Image titles
you will enjoy reading

➤ THE THRESHOLD OF GLORY
Compiled by Dotty Schmitt.
What does it mean to experience the "glory of God"? How does it come? These women of God have crossed that threshold, and it changed not only their ministries but also their very lives! Here Dotty Schmitt and Sue Ahn, Bonnie Chavda, Pat Chen, Dr. Flo Ellers, Brenda Kilpatrick, and Varle Rollins teach about God's glorious presence and share how it transformed their lives.
ISBN 0-7684-2044-X

➤ ONLY BELIEVE
by Don Stewart.
Who was A.A. Allen, John Dowie, Maria Woodworth-Etter, and William Branham? Who were these and the many other people who picked up the mantle of the healing evangelist in the twentieth century? What was their legacy? Don Stewart, who was mentored by A.A. Allen and had contact with most of his contemporaries in this widespread movement, gives an inside look into their lives and ministries. This incredible, firsthand witness account of the events and people who have shaped our current Christian heritage will astound you with how God takes frail, human vessels, pours out His anointing, and enables them to do mighty exploits for Him!
ISBN 1-56043-340-X

➤ ENCOUNTERS WITH A SUPERNATURAL GOD
by Jim W. and Michal Ann Goll.
The Golls know that angels are real. They have firsthand experience with supernatural angelic encounters. In this book you'll read and learn about angels and supernatural manifestations of God's Presence—and the real encounters that both Jim and Michal Ann have had! As the founders of Ministry to the Nations and speakers and teachers, they share that God wants to be intimate friends with His people. Go on an adventure with the Golls and find out if God has a supernatural encounter for you!
ISBN 1-56043-199-7

Available at your local Christian bookstore.

For more information and sample chapters, visit www.reapernet.com